KNOWLEDGE LINKS

Innovation in university-business partnerships

by Stephen Lissenburgh and Rebecca Harding

INSTITUTE FOR PUBLIC POLICY RESEARCH

INSTITUTE FOR PUBLIC POLICY RESEARCH

30-32 Southampton St
London WC2E 7RA
Tel: 0171 470 6100
Fax: 0171 470 6111
postmaster@ippr.org.uk
www.ippr.org.uk
Registered charity 800065

The Institute for Public Policy Research is an independent charity whose purpose is to contribute to public understanding of social, economic and political questions through research, discussion and publication. It was established in 1988 by leading figures in the academic, business and trade-union communities to provide an alternative to the free market think tanks.

IPPR's research agenda reflects the challenges facing Britain and Europe. Current programmes cover the areas of economic and industrial policy, Europe, governmental reform, human rights, defence, social policy, the environment and media issues.

Besides its programme of research and publication, IPPR also provides a forum for political and trade union leaders, academic experts and those from business, finance, government and the media, to meet and discuss issues of common concern.

Production & design by **EMPHASIS**
ISBN 1 86030 104 5
© IPPR 2000

Contents

Acknowledgements

The authors would like to thank all those people who assisted us with the research, and in particular the following:

The members of the advisory committee: Gerry Holtham, formerly Director of IPPR and now at Norwich Union Investment Management, who also initiated the study; Professor Kumar Bhattacharyya of Warwick Manufacturing Group; Sir Nicholas Monck; Professor Paul Geroski of London Business School; Ken Mayhew of the University of Oxford; and Sheila Watson; who read drafts of the chapters and gave us very helpful advice on the content and scope of the study.

Andrea Westall at IPPR, who did most of the background research for Chapter 1 and who, along with IPPR colleagues Peter Robinson and Prema Gurunathan, provided detailed comments and suggestions on the final draft. Helena Scott at IPPR did much to improve the presentation of the final manuscript.

Professor Martin Betts of the University of Salford and Professor Mike Sellars of the University of Sheffield, who were particularly helpful in arranging access to university staff and company personnel involved in collaborative research.

Nick Matthews and Tom Goodwin, with whom we had useful discussions on various aspects of the research and who were helpful in arranging interviews with Warwick Manufacturing Group staff and their industrial partners.

Professor Keith Pavitt who provided invaluable contacts at the outset of this research. Thanks are also due to Dr Ulrich Schmoch and Dr Hans-Willy Hohn for their assistance in putting together the German and American cases. The Fraunhofer Technology Development Groups provided unlimited access to their data and daily operations, but in particular, thanks are due to Harald Egner and to Dr Andreas Leverman for their co-operation and patience.

The study was funded by the Warwick Manufacturing Group, to whom grateful thanks are extended.

About the authors

Stephen Lissenburgh is Principal Research Fellow at the Policy Studies Institute. He was a Research Fellow at IPPR when working on this study.

Rebecca Harding is a Senior Fellow at SPRU, University of Sussex and a Research Associate at the IPPR. She has had international experience in teaching, research and policy consultancy in the area of innovation management, science and technology policy and, most recently, venture capital.

Summary

The UK has an excellent science base but is widely perceived as having a relatively poor record in technological innovation. Higher education institutions and other public sector research organisations have an important role to play in improving this situation. This report argues for changes in the culture, organisation and attitudes of universities so that they have the capacity and incentives to commercialise research and engage with business in making the journey from discovery to innovation and in improving existing products, services and processes.

This report illustrates the gains from greater knowledge links between universities and business by examining case studies of interaction, both from the UK and abroad, and drawing out the generic features of successful collaboration. It outlines a number of new initiatives designed to foster business-university partnerships, by:

- developing ways of evaluating and accrediting work done by universities with industry through a separate evaluation mechanism, which would complement the Research Assessment Exercise and the Teaching Quality Assessment.

- replicating the cluster working party exercise on biotechnology to cover a number of medium-tech sectors such as engineering, with a view to identifying nascent clusters in particular areas of the country and investigating ways of supporting their development.

- developing a system of regional and sectoral Centres of Excellence in the UK which would provide the opportunity to both widen and deepen the existing matrix of university-industry links.

- developing proposals for a National Innovation Agency (NIA), which would have responsibility for defining and coordinating UK innovation policy, particularly the most effective exploitation of the science base. As well as stimulating the demand for innovation, the NIA would co-ordinate the different policies concerned with science-industry interaction and spread best practice between initiatives. It would seek to rationalise what is widely seen as a confusing and overlapping series of smaller schemes promoting applied and collaborative work. Such an organisation, combined with the other policy recommendations made by this report and existing best practice, should stimulate more effective business-university partnerships.

Research policy and industry-academia interactions

Chapter 1 examines the reasons for links between higher education institutions and the business sector, assesses evidence on current levels of university-industry interaction in the UK and how these compare to other industrialised economies, critically evaluates the current policy framework for the encouragement of knowledge links and suggests possible areas for policy development.

There is a plethora of government programmes and initiatives designed to encourage collaboration between universities and industry in the UK but, despite these, the overall level of interaction is not high by international standards and is rather low compared to the US and Germany. The matrix of policies developed by the Conservatives, especially after 1993, has been added to and extended by the Labour government's 1998 White Paper, *Our Competitive Future: Building the Knowledge Driven Economy*, which contains a number of new initiatives designed to increase the incentives for both universities and firms to form productive partnerships. These new initiatives are along the right lines and represent a keenly required move towards creating an innovation policy and not just a science and technology policy, but are rather too piecemeal to bring about a dramatic change in the UK's innovation performance. The conclusion to this report contains policy recommendations for more radical change, as well as for enhancement of existing programmes.

Pharmaceuticals and biotechnology

These two sectors have been particularly successful in the UK, since they both spend large amounts on research and development and university-industry partnerships are dominant features of the sectoral landscape. In particular, there is a detailed look at two examples of collaboration – the links developed by the Edward Jenner Institute for Vaccine Research; and the Medical Research Council's (MRC) collaborative work, with special focus being placed on its Collaborative Centre at Mill Hill. The Jenner Institute and MRC Collaborative Centre are examples of intermediate institutions, in that they are relatively autonomous from both the science base and the business sector but provide a link between them. The research intensity of pharmaceuticals and biotechnology means that some of the specific features of these institutions are not transferable but there are lessons to be learned.

Particularly in hi-tech, but in other areas as well, the importance of risk-spreading through consortium, or partnership, funding cannot be over-stated. This is because 'blue sky' research is unpredictable in terms of its commercial potential. Projects may take years to build up commercial momentum, if, indeed, they ever do. But through partnership funding structures (evident in particular in the Jenner Institute), a critical mass of research develops from which the chances of commercial exploitation are maximised.

Collaborative research should focus on the core interests of the academic scientists in the first instance since this guarantees the innovative quality of the output, but the end objective of commercialisation should not be forgotten. At the Jenner Institute, this trade-off is effected through the participation of industrial scientists in research projects, thereby ensuring that any commercial potential is identified.

Similarly, participation of industrial scientists in research ensures that the 'translator role' is not lost – in other words, there are appropriate qualified personnel to carry the research results back into industrial applications.

Projects in both cases are managed professionally.

Engineering and materials

In contrast to pharmaceuticals and biotechnology, engineering and materials are two sectors in which the UK's competitive record in recent decades has been poor. If the government is to achieve its policy objectives in these areas, then it must find mechanisms for stimulating them, not least because, along with the rest of manufacturing, they still account for a sizeable proportion of UK exports, employment and output. Chapter 3 analyses the Warwick Manufacturing Group (WMG) and the Sheffield Materials Forum (SMF), university-based organisations that have formed a number of collaborative partnerships with companies in the engineering and materials sectors. WMG and SMF are attached to academic departments in their respective universities, but act as intermediate institutions providing a formalised link between the science base and their business partners. These partnerships have encouraged the types of incremental innovation in production process development which are appropriate for applied technology sectors and some important lessons can be drawn from their experiences.

In both cases, support at a university level for greater links with industry was substantial and essential to making the partnership projects work. At Warwick, this support was evident through the University's tolerance of industry-standard pay-scales and terms and conditions, while at Sheffield, support at the highest level has guaranteed the effective development of networks.

Both universities had dynamic, entrepreneurial academics in charge of the industry-university links which provided the drive behind the projects.

Overcoming cultural resistance on the part of industry to the activities traditionally conducted by universities has been achieved at both institutions through education and training, through professional project management and, critically, through the development of substantial networks of small and large companies from the local area. These networks serve the purpose of building trust, sharing experience and of generating project ideas and income.

The Warwick example in particular illustrates the importance of providing adequate rewards and returns for staff in taking a post within a university in the first place and, once there, in pursuing industry-relevant activities. The Manufacturing Group pays industry competitive salaries and has clear career paths. This type of staff development potential provides incentives aside from the normal RAE accredited publications which mean that their industry-based work is equally valued.

Construction and packaging

As with engineering and materials, the scope for innovation within the construction and packaging sectors is incremental rather than radical in nature. These two sectors are ones in which firms have low technological capability and there is very little demand for interaction with universities. Chapter 4, however, analyses the Construct IT Centre of Excellence, an organisation based at the University of Salford that works with the construction industry, and the White Rose Faraday Partnership for Enhanced Packaging Technology, based at the universities of Leeds, Sheffield and York, both of which have formed partnerships with companies aimed at encouraging innovation in product and process development.

The case studies make it possible to draw the following lessons regarding factors that encourage successful university-industry interaction:

● Where centres are based in universities there is a need for a supportive environment at the highest level. This refers both to the need for 'support in principle' and, critically for more pragmatic support in the form of adequate incentive structures to encourage staff in an academic environment.

● Both the Construct IT and White Rose projects re-inforce the contention that networks are important in the development of trust and understanding between partners and in developing appropriate research projects. However, it is important that these networks are not simply with R&D personnel. The White Rose Partnership had contacts predominantly with R&D managers rather than with managing directors of local businesses. The effect was to restrict the commercial opportunities offered by partnership research.

● The importance of education and training in breaking down the cultural barriers should not be under-played. The role of teaching is central to Construct IT and extra projects and networks have developed as a result. Indeed, a major weakness of the White Rose Partnership was that it did not at the time of the research have obvious links into the teaching function of its partner universities which acted as a brake on informal networking activities. Policy should thus take into account the need for explicit links into the teaching function in order to enhance industry-university links.

Communications

The university-industry collaborations referred to above have mostly involved firms in manufacturing. It is well known, however, that the relative importance of this sector has declined markedly since at least the

1970s, both in terms of output and employment shares. In contrast, the service sector has come to account for an increasingly large proportion of output and employment and indeed, dominates the economy. For this reason, Chapter 5 analyses the Virtual Centre of Excellence in Mobile and Personal Communications (Mobile VCE), a collaborative partnership between more than twenty of the world's most prominent mobile communications companies and seven UK universities each having long standing specialist expertise in relevant areas. Analysis of Mobile VCE suggests the following:

- Its status as a limited company, with the associated allocation of legal responsibilities, ensures that the Centre is managed in a professional way, which is partly why it is able to attract high quality, innovative businesses to its industrial membership. It may be that, once university-industry collaboration involves the levels of industrial funding received by Mobile VCE, management structures more reminiscent of the private sector are appropriate.

- The main reason why Mobile VCE has high fees for corporate membership is because substantial demand exists in the mobile and personal communications industry for research which may promote technological innovation. The industry's products have a high technological component and being able to understand and carry out technological innovation is essential to firms' ability to compete in the sector. While it is difficult to replicate these levels of demand across the board, this does show the importance of encouraging firms to appreciate the need for innovation and to compete on product quality.

- The idea of creating a virtual centre, whereby the expertise of leading universities in the sector is pooled and the Centre does not have a physical base, is one of potentially wide applicability. It is comparatively rare in any industrial sector for there to be one, or even two universities, which have sufficient expertise to be able to sustain a substantial amount of collaboration with industry. Pulling in experts from a range of universities creates a critical mass and range of intellectual ability that is able to carry out a detailed and varied programme of research.

International comparisons

With British policy arguably still seeking direction in the area of technology transfer, the extent to which alternative models can be imported into a British context needs to be assessed. Chapter Six reviews the German and American systems and discusses their transferability. In the German case, particular attention is focused on the Fraunhofer Gesellschaft, intermediate institutions that enable business to access knowledge from the science base. The US case study highlights the role of Centres of Excellence, which cluster around leading regional universities and typically involve university-industry research centres (intermediate institutions), research institutes, industrial research laboratories and/or industrial production, testing facilities (for example hospitals or clinics), a developed regional product market, access to a highly skilled workforce and, often, a risk-friendly venture capital environment. The analyses in Chapter 6 suggest that:

- Encouraging clusters of innovation with public and private funds in regional centres has produced dividends for the US technology transfer system. Evidence of such clusters is emerging in Britain too, but more could be done to stimulate these.

- Ultimately, both the US and the German cases point to the usefulness of formal and informal networks, of education and training and of project management according to industrial principles in industry-HEI collaboration.

- Neither country faces the cultural difficulties experienced in the UK since partnership structures have evolved as part of the economic structures in the two countries. Even so, both systems have mechanisms to ensure that any mistrust is limited through networks and through partnership programmes. These are the basic lessons for British policy.

Conclusions and policy recommendations

Chapter 7 synthesises material from the research by developing the generic characteristics of successful collaborations between industry and the public sector research base. These are as follows:

- *Creating a demand for innovation*

  The most fundamental barrier to the creation of university-industry links is firms' scepticism about the ability of such links to improve their business. The case studies, and especially the experience of WMG, illustrate what universities can do to stimulate the demand for innovation and knowledge links. Key factors in this process are education and research synergies, but also of importance is the need to demonstrate quickly to firms the current and potential benefits of collaboration. This is best done by short-term contract research that has a good chance of early pay-off. Once this has been done successfully, and the company becomes more confident in the university's ability to deliver, there is a better chance that they will fund more speculative, pre-competitive work in the future.

- *University infrastructure*

  Most of the examples of successful links with business uncovered by this research have been found in universities with a strong institutional commitment to collaboration with industry. Where universities are keen to encourage links with industry and to expand their economic development role, they should give consideration to the following factors: altering their mission statements to give economic development explicit consideration alongside academic research and teaching; concentrating decision-making in a stream-lined, centralised body but then allowing relative autonomy to those units and centres it supports, along the lines of the Warwick model; promoting a culture in which collaboration with industry is regarded as mainstream and good practice.

- *Incentive structures*

  Academics are discouraged from engaging in applied work with industry because it does not lead to career enhancement in the way that excellence in academic research and teaching are inclined to do. In order to address this problem, universities need to create a legitimate and recognised career framework for academics, which rewards and gives status for work in applications areas, complementary to the framework for those following careers in scholarly research and teaching.

- *Intermediate institutions*

  The research suggests that intermediate institutions, which are relatively autonomous from both the science base and the business sector but provide a link between them, are in a better position to undertake large-scale collaboration with industry than universities which seek to engage in industrial links without forming intermediate institutions of this type. This is partly because intermediate institutions are more adept at performing or facilitating the 'translator' role, whereby findings from the science base inform industrial practice by ensuring that the requirements of those at the 'development' end are understood by those at the 'research' end, and vice-versa. In addition, such institutions often gather expertise from more than one university, so they can achieve a critical mass that creates more valuable interaction with industry than would be possible otherwise.

- *Industrial relevance and industrial champions*

  Many of the centres we examined were very successful in carefully involving their industrial members in the formulation of research programmes, so they could lay genuine claim to being industry-led. This is an important ingredient of successful university-industry collaboration, especially where firms are sceptical about the value of working with universities and suspect that universities are only interested in their own research agendas. This scepticism can be similarly overcome by 'industrial champions', key figures from the industrial sectors involved in the collaboration who transfer their enthusiasm for it to their business contacts.

- *Education/research synergies*

  There are strong synergies between university-business research collaboration and the provision of industrially relevant, post-experience education. It was through the provision of such education that WMG, in particular, was able to create demand for its research capabilities: those students who passed through its courses became aware of the potential of collaboration and also developed the skills to make it work. There is little to be gained from research links if company personnel do not have the ability to absorb technological innovation.

- *Managing the entrepreneurial vision*

  Carrying out successful links with industry requires the key players on the university side to have a wide range of skills and to carry out a number of challenging activities: they need to have an awareness of the transferable aspects of the knowledge base but also sufficient entrepreneurial vision to see the possibilities for commercial exploitation. This ability to 'look both ways' is uncommon but is an essential requirement. Professional project management skills are also of fundamental importance.

- *Regional clusters*

  The case studies produced some evidence to suggest that universities can be the foci of 'clusters' of firms from particular industrial groupings. Facilitating the development of regional clusters brings benefits for both firms and universities, making it possible for technological innovations to be spread amongst a much wider range of firms than would be possible if such clusters did not exist. The consequences of this for productivity and profitability are clear. This industrial learning is facilitated further by the development of inter-firm networks. For universities, developing industrial clubs is an essential part of building up the research client base and breaking down the barriers of scepticism which inhibit the formation of knowledge links. These regional clusters were found in medium-tech as well as hi-tech sectors.

While the conclusions outlined above show what universities and firms can learn from the research to encourage interaction, the remainder of Chapter 7 outlines the policy changes which government could bring about to provide it with further support and encouragement. The policy recommendations are divided into those which advocate enhancement of existing policies and provision, changes in the criteria by which potential projects are assessed under current programmes, and new initiatives.

Enhancement of existing policies and provision

- *Basic science*

  The case studies showed that business demand for collaboration with the public sector research base is greatest where university researchers are able to access the latest developments in basic science. It is not an overstatement to say that a high quality, curiosity-driven science base is the lifeblood of university-industry interaction. As such, this report welcomes the additional support given to the science base by the Comprehensive Spending Review, but suggests that this should be the beginning of enhanced provision and not the final statement.

- *Higher Education Reach-out to Business and the Community (HEROBEC) Fund*

Jointly created by the DTI, DfEE and HEFCE in 1999, the HEROBEC fund is for activities that will increase the capability of higher education institutions to interact with business to promote technology and knowledge transfer. As such, it provides financial support for the type of activities which this research has shown to encourage innovation and improvements in business performance. A total of £11 million is earmarked for the Fund in 1999-2000 for English institutions, rising to £22 million in 2002-03. In similar moves, Scottish Enterprise and SHEFCE will devote an extra £11 million per year over the next three years to these issues. While HEROBEC is clearly a welcome development, the scale of funding would need to be considerably higher to have an appreciable impact on universities' ability to work effectively with industry, especially in relation to English institutions. At the very least, the funding for English institutions should be equivalent pro rata to that provided in Scotland, which suggests the HEROBEC budget should rise to about £100 million by 2002-03.

- *Faraday Partnerships*

It was announced in the Competitiveness White Paper that the DTI would be supporting the Faraday Programme introduced by the EPSRC in 1997, to the extent that the number of Faraday Partnerships would rise over the next two or three years from its present level of four to about twenty. This makes the Partnerships an important method of encouraging university-industry links to facilitate technology transfer. At the core of the Faraday model are research and training organisations (RTOs), which play the crucial 'translator' role in linking firms with the science base. While the basic structure of the Faraday model is supported by this research, its essential ingredients are present in some of the intermediate institutions we have looked at, even where an RTO is not involved. Especially in the cases of Warwick Manufacturing Group and the Medical Research Council Collaborative Centre, the 'translator' role is carried out effectively by staff from within these organisations. This suggests that, as DTI invites new applications for Faraday Partnerships, it should include proposals that allow for the intermediate institution role to be played by institutions other than RTOs.

- *Translators*

This research has demonstrated the crucial role played by 'translators', university staff who can 'look both ways' when facilitating knowledge transfer between universities and industry. Policies which help university staff to develop the entrepreneurial skills required by this task would increase the supply of potential 'translators'. In this respect, the Science Enterprise Challenge, which has created eight enterprise centres at leading UK universities, will have an important role to play. The aim of the centres is to equip scientists and engineers with entrepreneurship and business skills to develop the transfer and exploitation of knowledge and know-how. The programme was introduced by the Competitiveness White Paper and £25 million of funding was spread among the eight centres. As with the HEROBEC fund, this programme is well-conceived but conservatively funded, in relation both to the number of centres created and the support made available to each. A four-fold increase in funding and a doubling of the centres supported would produce a more adequate supply of translators. The highly regarded Teaching Company Scheme could also have its 'translation' role made more explicit.

- *Changes in assessment criteria*

The research suggests that government programmes designed to encourage collaboration between universities and business could be made more effective if certain factors were given more weight than at present when funding proposals are being assessed. This applies to HEROBEC, Faraday Partnerships, Science Enterprise Challenge and all of the other programmes described in the chapter on industry/academia partnerships.

- *University mission statements and infrastructural support*

  In view of the finding that strong commitment to the economic development function at the university level is an important determinant of successful interaction with business, it is recommended that the content of university mission statements and tangible evidence of support for collaboration from a senior level within universities be given more weighting in the assessment of funding proposals.

- *Involvement of industrial champions*

  The research suggests that the chances of university-industry interaction having a lasting effect on business performance are greatly enhanced if industrial 'champions' are used to involve senior managers in the collaboration. Universities that are able to demonstrate access to such industrial champions should be given credit for this in assessment criteria.

- *Education/research synergies*

  Education and training played an important role in several of the case studies in ensuring that companies had willingness to engage in research collaboration with universities and the ability to implement any technological innovations which emerged from this. The ability to demonstrate such linkages should be used to assess whether universities would provide good value for any public money they should receive to encourage interaction.

- *Links between science departments and business schools*

  The research noted that some of the most successful US examples of university-industry links came about where university business or management schools and science or engineering departments had come together to form a multi-disciplinary centre best able to deliver effective collaboration with business. UK universities have been much less inclined to do this: of the eight centres created by

Science Enterprise Challenge, only one was a formal collaboration between a business school and science department. It is recommended that the formation of such collaborations be given due weight when assessing funding proposals.

New initiatives

- *Accreditation of applied work*

The creation of HEROBEC provides a source of funding which can kickstart university-industry interactions in those institutions that make successful bids, but there is a wider issue of the appropriate assessment and evaluation of the broad range of applied work which takes place in universities. It was generally felt by those researchers involved in the case study institutions that the Research Assessment Exercise (RAE) does not give sufficient credit to applied work carried out with industry. The best way to rectify this is not to remove the current bias of the RAE towards basic and strategic research, since this helps to maintain the quality of basic science, but instead to develop ways of evaluating and accrediting work done with industry through a separate evaluation mechanism. This should evaluate processes and mechanisms rather than direct outcomes, in much the same way as the Teaching Quality Assessment. By providing a 'badge of quality' it could be used as a vehicle for increasing the status of applied work and could also be part of the evaluation criteria for the award of HEROBEC funds.

- *Cluster working parties*

The national and international case studies produced some evidence to suggest that universities can be the foci of 'clusters' of firms from particular industrial groupings. A notable feature of the regional clusters observed in this research is their existence in medium-tech rather than hi-tech sectors. It is recommended, therefore, that the cluster working party exercise on biotechnology, convened by the government early in 1999, be replicated for a number of medium-tech sectors, with a view to identifying nascent clusters in particular areas of the country and investigating ways of supporting their development.

- *Regional and sectoral centres of excellence*

  Much of the analysis reported in this research points to the need for the development of collaborative centres which bring together a number of key players in the innovation process. Developing a system of regional and sectoral Centres of Excellence in the UK would provide the opportunity to both widen and deepen the existing matrix of university-industry links. Bringing together a wider group of institutions and types of research capacity would mean that a greater range of expertise could be applied to the task of improving firms' innovative capacity. Adequate public funding of basic research carried out by the Centres and sliding-scale public funding of applied research, where larger companies would fund all or nearly all of projects from which they benefited but SME-related projects would receive public support, would help to deepen the relationships. The government should aim to create ten such centres by 2002, each receiving an average of £10 million funding in the 2000-2002 period.

- *National Innovation Agency (NIA)*

  The research also points to the need for a macro-level attempt to raise the profile of innovation. This is best made by a government agency charged with the task of defining and co-ordinating UK innovation policy particularly to ensure the most effective exploitation of the science base. As such, it should be part of the DTI but relatively autonomous from it. As well as stimulating the demand for innovation, the NIA would co-ordinate the different elements of innovation policy outlined and suggested by this report, and introduce mechanisms through which the work of different institutions – Faraday Partnerships, Regional and Sectoral Centres of Excellence and other collaborative centres – could be used to inform that of the others. At the same time as co-ordinating these large programmes, it would need to rationalise what is widely seen as a confusing and overlapping series of smaller schemes promoting applied and collaborative work. Such an organisation, combined with the other policy recommendations made by this report and existing best practice, would stimulate more effective knowledge links.

Introduction

The UK has an excellent science base but is widely perceived as having a relatively poor record in technological innovation. Higher education institutions and other public sector research organisations have an important role to play in improving this situation. This report argues for changes in the culture, organisation and attitudes of universities so that they have the capacity and incentives to commercialise research and engage with business in making the journey from discovery to innovation and in improving existing products, services and processes.

Searching for the roots of Britain's innovation problem by focusing solely on universities, however, would provide an unbalanced account. With the exception of a few hi-tech sectors, notably pharmaceuticals, British industry has not carried out technological innovation at the rate required to compete effectively in the global economy. The reasons for this are multi-faceted, but a key distinction between pharmaceuticals and other sectors is in the extent to which they conform to the 'linear model' of innovation. In pharmaceuticals, scientific input determines a large proportion of the product's value and close links with the science base are required to access the latest developments. In the applied technology sectors however, such as engineering, scientific advancement tends to be more piecemeal and the benefits of innovation less obvious. This is because they lie more often than not in production process development – an uncertain and incremental process which may or may not yield productivity increases.

It is the 'fuzzy' and uncertain nature of the innovation process in many industrial sectors which tends to inhibit links with the science base, as it is less than obvious that benefits will ensue. It is these sectors which are most in need of revitalisation if British business is to close the performance gap with comparable countries, in terms of both productivity and its ability to produce innovative products and create high-value services.

This report hopes to illustrate the gains from greater knowledge links between universities and business by examining examples of interaction, both from the UK and abroad, and drawing out the generic features of successful collaboration. The study on which it is based looks at business-university partnerships that involve both research and education, and covers a range of sectors that runs from the science-led hi-tech of pharmaceuticals and biotechnology to applied technology groupings like engineering and materials, and low-tech industries like construction and packaging. It also draws lessons from a high-value-added services sector – personal and mobile communications – in which European companies are world leaders, and considers the wider experience of two countries, Germany and the US, which can boast very different but highly effective models of university-business collaboration.

The overall picture in the UK, however, remains one where the inhibitions of both universities and firms have contributed to low levels of interaction between the two, especially in the applied technology sectors. This is despite the existence of a plethora of government programmes and initiatives designed to encourage collaboration, many of which were spawned by the Conservative Government's Competitiveness White Paper, *Realising Our Potential*, in 1993. The matrix of policies developed by the Conservatives has been added to and extended by the Labour's Government's 1998 White Paper, *Our Competitive Future: Building the Knowledge-Driven Economy*, which contains a number of new initiatives designed to increase the incentives for both universities and firms to form productive partnerships. Notable amongst these are the Higher Education Reach-out to Business (HEROBEC) fund, which rewards universities for strategies and activities that enhance interaction with business, and the Science Enterprise Challenge, which has created eight enterprise centres at leading UK universities. These new initiatives are along the right lines and represent a greatly required move towards creating an innovation policy and not just a science and technology policy, but are rather too piecemeal to bring about a dramatic change in the UK's innovation performance. The conclusion to this report contains policy recommendation for more radical change.

Structure of the report

The research has three main elements.

- A critical evaluation of the current policy framework for the encouragement of links between business and the public sector research base. This is done in Chapter 1.

- A series of case studies, which take a detailed look at examples of university-business interaction. These cover the sectors of pharmaceuticals and biotechnology, engineering and materials, construction, packaging and communications. These are examined in Chapters 2-5.

- Chapter 6 looks at comparable German and US models of interaction, while Chapter 7 draws conclusions and outlines the policy recommendations.

1. Research policy and industry-academia interactions

The Government placed great store by creating a 'knowledge economy' in its Competitiveness White Paper (1998) and, as part of this, has developed policies to enhance university-industry links and university spin-outs. Industrialists and policy-makers alike bemoan the 'unexploited potential' of universities as generators of innovative ideas which, logically, could be turned into viable business propositions. They point to the example of the US economy where commercially viable University-Industry Research Centres (UIRCs) are part of the industrial landscape. Similarly, in their Regional Economic Strategies, all of the newly established English Regional Development Agencies (RDAs) have stated as clear objectives the integration of their region's universities with business. They have also stressed closer co-operation between universities and business in the development of regional innovation strategies.

With the obvious exception of a small number of hi-tech industries, however, relations between universities and business in Britain are neither uniformly good nor even productive. Their interactions have been historically underpinned by a mutual distrust of each other's values and beliefs. Neither group naturally learns from the other either in terms of methodology or in terms of outcome. Accusations such as, 'That would never happen if they had to run like businesses' are all-too-frequently thrown at universities, while equally vitriolic and scornful comments are returned from academics, for example, 'Well, he would say that, wouldn't he – he's in *business*.'[1] This polemic is even reflected in the way in which universities' work has traditionally been assessed and rewarded. The Research Assessment Exercise (RAE), running since the early 1990s, rewards academic excellence through publication in internationally renowned journals. Consultancy and 'outreach' activities, such as industrial placements and the Teaching Company Scheme (TCS) are not recognised as contributing to the process of generating this 'academic excellence'.

Despite this, the pervasive assumption that enhancing co-operation and collaboration between universities and business is necessarily a 'good thing' is gathering pace. Universities have a key role in technology transfer and innovation, as is shown by examples outside the UK given in Chapter 6. But equally importantly, they have substantial, and as yet under-utilised, potential in generating business ideas and, hence, growth. There is evidence of best practice, as is illustrated by this research, albeit on a heavily regional basis. Where the relationship works well it has rested on a sea change in attitudes towards university-industry links.

Nowhere is this need for cultural change more recognised than at a policy level. Senior officials describe the current system as 'embryonic' and Department of Trade and Industry (DTI) literature itself argues that, 'If an exchange of benefits is to take place on a sustained basis, it is necessary to behave in a way that builds a bridge between the academic institution and its non-academic partner, each with its own set of values and way of organising itself' (DTI, 1998a).

But the difficulties in creating this greater understanding should not be under-estimated. While platitudes about the inherent attractions of greater links help to raise public consciousness about the potential embodied in greater university-industry interactions, without hard financial incentives it is very difficult to bring either side to the table. This, then, is where policy has a role, and equally where policy faces its major challenge. Universities as a rule do not turn down offers of money and view the opportunity to create centres and units as exciting. But in order that companies, particularly small and medium-sized enterprises (SMEs), use these centres, they have to see the potential to increase their profit margins. In the short term, this may not be immediately apparent and some form of incentivisation may be appropriate while the system is established.

This chapter examines in detail existing links between universities and business. It assesses the rationale behind enhancing links between academia and industry at a policy and at a practical level and looks at the mechanisms by which these links are effected through current policies and practice. It concludes with an assessment of current structures and policies.

Rationale for enhancing the links

Since the mutual benefits of co-operation between Higher Education Institutions (HEIs) and business are at present implicit rather than explicit, there is, therefore, a real need to explore the rationale for developing their interaction.

Government policy, as has been mentioned in the introduction aims to address the perceived productivity gap experienced by the UK by turning more attention than has hitherto been given to the role of technological innovation where there are both demand and supply side weaknesses. On the one hand, many companies do not appreciate the need for innovation, showing little willingness or ability to access and utilise technological opportunities. On the other hand, there are those institutions, such as universities, which have a wealth of technological and scientific capability but are not adequately organised or provided with sufficient incentives to collaborate effectively with firms in the delivery of innovative change.

This lack of technological innovation is regarded as holding back UK productivity performance in two distinct areas. First, a slow rate of product development and a concentration on low quality products has long been recognised as a weakness of the UK economy. This 'low skills/low quality equilibrium' (Finegold and Soskice 1988) means that the lack of an appropriately trained workforce exacerbates a pre-existing tendency for firms to follow low value-added product development strategies. More recent case study and econometric research would suggest that UK companies follow lower specification product strategies than companies in many comparator countries (Prais, 1995; Oulton 1996; Buxton *et al*, 1998; Porter 1998). Second, there are perceptible weaknesses in process development evident from the DTI's own research which also leads to comparative weaknesses in productivity (DTI 1998b:39).

There are two key questions here:

- What is the role of HEIs in innovation and technology transfer generally?

- What is the role of HEIs in generating high quality business propositions and, hence, higher productivity, product and process innovation and growth?

These issues can be represented very simply in a linear model, as shown in Figure 1.1. As the figure shows, universities have traditionally concentrated on basic scientific research and, largely amongst the 'new' universities, some applied research. The RAE, referred to above, rewards this activity, particularly advances contained in the 'Basic Science' category (i.e. disciplinary advances). While some basic research is conducted in industrial laboratories, product and process application is more commonly conducted by companies. The assumption underpinning this model, as it has developed over time, is that knowledge transfers from the science base through personnel (for example, students leaving universities) and through publications.

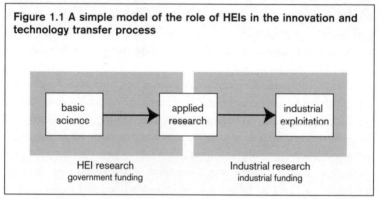

Figure 1.1 A simple model of the role of HEIs in the innovation and technology transfer process

It would be over-simplistic, however, to suggest that this model is uniformly appropriate for generating effective transfer of technology and innovation or of creating good business opportunities. Indeed, the model itself mitigates against this transfer since it assumes a linear and one way process rather than an iterative process of interaction between universities and business. Nor does it reflect the way in which universities themselves have developed over the last 20 years as the quantity of public funding for basic scientific research has declined and as they have been obliged by financial necessity to seek funding from industrial sources.

A more appropriate model might be that illustrated in Figure 1.2 which shows the iterative relationship between HEIs and industry which is necessary if partnership projects, innovation and technology transfer are to be effective. It clearly distinguishes 'partnership' links, such as the Teaching Company Scheme (TCS) and student placement programmes, or joint research leading to published outputs. The success of these projects can be measured through numbers of TCS graduates or numbers of papers and projects. The interaction is relatively low risk and is effective as a means of developing mutual understanding between the two parties as well as creating incremental innovations.

Below the central arrow in Figure 2 is the technology transfer and commercial exploitation of linkages between academia and industry. The risks involved with these types of 'business' projects are considerably higher and the returns often accrue over a longer period of time. They involve basic research and radical innovation and, hence, have more commercial potential. These are the projects which are necessarily more suitable to policy instruments such as 'University Challenge' (the Government's seed corn fund to encourage university spin-outs). The results are measured through patents, through Intellectual Property Rights (IPR) agreements and through numbers of university spin-outs.

Ultimately projects on both sides of the arrow have the potential to generate product and process innovations, higher productivity and economic growth. Partnership projects often focus on specific product or process technologies and often have as their objective, prompted through public sector funding bodies such as the Engineering and Physical Science Research Council (EPSRC), the sharing of best practice amongst networks of practitioners. Projects such as the CIRCA[2] or the CoPS[3] programmes in Sussex are typical examples of how such partnerships disseminate best practice, build understanding of innovative processes and ultimately assist companies in reducing costs. Similarly, the higher risk spin-out projects have the potential to establish highly innovative, high growth companies in new markets and to enhance the development of clusters in a particular technological area, as is seen with biotechnology in Cambridge, advanced manufacturing in Warwick and rail technology in Derbyshire.

Disclaimer: putting university inputs in perspective

A recent survey of hi-tech firms by the DTI and the Science Policy Research Unit (SPRU) (cited in POST, 1998) found that Intellectual Property Rights agreements and contacts with the science base were less important to innovation than were the supply chain, internal qualified scientists and engineers and Research and Technology Organisations (RTOs). When looking at sources of new ideas, most came from in-house (75 per cent of cases). The same survey noted that external sources of new ideas (Table 1.1) originated primarily from customers and the supply chain followed by the knowledge pool, including public business support services and the science and engineering base (SEB). For SMEs, RTOs are just as, if not more, important than the SEB (POST, 1998). A survey of the largest manufacturing and industrial firms in Europe, the PACE Report 1995, concluded that the main source of technical knowledge was the technical analysis of a competitor's products followed by suppliers and customers (cited in Martin and Salter, 1996).

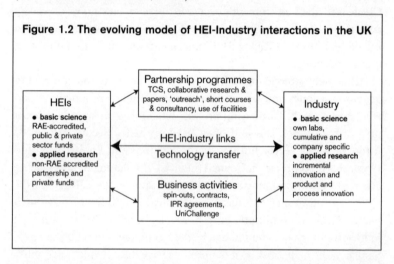

Figure 1.2 The evolving model of HEI-Industry interactions in the UK

Table 1.1 The importance attributed to the assistance of external support groups in innovation

	Very useful	Useful	No use	Never used
Customers	45	44	5	6
Suppliers	33	56	5	6
Trade Associations	15	45	14	26
Consultants	9	40	23	28
TECs/LECs	7	27	17	50
Competitions	6	44	26	24
Chambers of Commerce	6	39	18	37
HEIs	6	25	18	51
Research Associations	5	22	17	55
Government Departments	4	33	26	37
Business Links	2	11	18	70
Business Clubs	1	6	18	75

Source: DTI/SPRU survey quoted in POST (1998)

Evidence on university-industry interactions

The UK's overall record on industrial funding of research and development (R&D) is not particularly good by international standards, being lower as a percentage of GDP than all other G7 countries apart from Canada and Italy in 1997 (see Table 1.2).[4] It was also lower than that of a number of other EU countries in that year, notably Sweden, but was close to the EU average.

Table 1.2 Financing of expenditures on R&D by business enterprise as a percentage of GDP

	1993	1995	1997
Canada	0.7	0.7	0.8
France	1.2	1.1	1.1[a]
Germany	1.5	1.4	1.4
Ireland	0.8	0.9	1.0
Italy	0.5	0.4	0.5
Japan	2.0	2.0	2.1[a]
Netherlands	0.9	1.0	1.0[a]
Spain	0.4	0.4	0.4
Sweden	2.1	2.4	2.6
UK	1.1	1.0	0.9
US	1.5	1.6	1.7
EU	1.0	1.0	1.0[a]

a = 1996

Source: OECD (1999), Science, Technology and Industry Scoreboard Table 3.2.2.

The UK's record is rather better when one considers evidence specifically on university-industry interactions. Table 1.3 shows the percentage share of business in the funding of research performed by higher education in the 1985-1997 period.

While the UK's figure fluctuates over the period, the 7.2 per cent share of business in higher education R&D in 1997 is higher than any country with the exception of Germany, which exhibits a strong record throughout 1985-97, and New Zealand, where business has achieved a relatively high share of higher education R&D spending much more recently. The US also scores quite highly. Considering Tables 1.2 and 1.3 together, the US and Germany amongst large economies have a good record both in business funding of R&D overall and business

Table 1.3 Percentage share of R&D performed in the higher education sector funded by business enterprise

	1985	1990	1995	1997
United States	3.8	4.7	5.8[b]	5.8
Japan	1.5	2.3	2.4[d]	2.4[b]
New Zealand		4.6	5.2[d]	9.4
France	1.9	4.9	3.2[c]	3.2[b]
Germany	5.9	7.8	7.5[b]	7.9
Italy	1.5	2.4	5.5[b]	3.8
Norway	5.0	4.7[a]	5.3	5.2
United Kingdom	5.2	7.6	6.2	7.2

a = 1992; b = 1996; c = 1994; d = 1993

Source: Senker, J (1999) *University Research Financing* report prepared for the OECD, SPRU Science and Technology Policy Research University of Sussex, February; and OECD Science, Technology and Industry Scoreboard 1999, Table 4.5.1.

funding of that R&D carried out in the higher education sector. These are the two countries whose knowledge transfer institutions are considered in detail in Chapter 6.

Despite the fact that the UK's record is perhaps less impressive overall than that of Germany and the US, in no sense should the potential importance of universities be under-played, particularly since many companies are unaware of the gains to be made by utilising external sources of advice (DTI 1998a). As Senker (1998) argues, the ability to use external sources depends on the presence of internal qualified scientists and technologists who know how to access available networks of knowledge. This is a particularly severe problem for SMEs. Yet, as innovations themselves become more complex, more multi-disciplinary and more fast-growing, the role of universities as external inputs to innovation becomes more important.

This, then, strikes at the heart of the cultural difficulties inherent to the interaction discussed above. The key is in changing the 'external behaviour' of both parties in order to derive mutual understanding (DTI 1998a). This involves a process of understanding each other's values. This may involve projects in the 'lower risk' categories in Figure 1.2 in the first instance.

There is evidence that such 'mutual learning' projects are increasing in importance:

- Joint paper publication has shown a steady increase and collaborative research is becoming more important to UK industry (Hicks and Katz 1996). In 1981, about 60 per cent of industry's UK collaborations were with a university partner and by 1994 that had risen to 75 per cent. It is not just collaborations between industry and academia that are increasing, there is a growing trend towards increased collaboration across institutions in general.

- There are sectoral differences in the use of industry-academia links for innovation and policy should take these into account. A report of three high-tech sectors, biotechnology, parallel computing and engineering ceramics by Faulkner and Senker (1995) concluded that the public science base contributes to innovation mostly through trained scientists and technologists and as a 'potent source of new knowledge'. Additionally, the number of informal links between academics and industry exceeds the number of formal interactions for all sectors.

It is important, then, that any university-industry partnership arrangements take account of the strengths of each party in order to accrue the expected mutual benefits. Evidence is patchy on this:

- Anecdotal evidence from the case studies conducted for this research suggests that some HEIs are offering very rudimentary courses such as basic computer skills. One has to ask whether this is the best use of highly-trained academic staff.

- It is not uniformly clear that this is actually what industry itself wants. In a survey of the largest manufacturing and industrial firms in Europe, the PACE Report of 1995, UK respondents stressed the importance of basic research over more applied areas. In evidence submitted by industrialists to William Waldegrave's White Paper *Realising Our Potential*, the majority did not want universities to shift their research to more applied work (Lyall, 1993). It is important to remember this in the drive towards 'greater relevance' of the science base and increased demand for academics to work with industry.

The importance of basic science to the UK economy

While the UK's record in business-funded R&D is less good than that of some leading economies, as shown by Tables 2 & 3, on most counts it looks as though the UK has a strong competitive position in scientific research:

- The UK is the research partner of choice in EU collaborative projects.

- On most measures of the quality of the science base we come second only to the US. The OST (1997) concluded from an analysis of numbers of scientific publications and citation levels across countries that with one per cent of the world's population, 5.5 per cent research effort, 8 per cent of publications and 9.1 per cent of all citations emanate from the UK.

However, there is some indication that this comparative strength is not sustainable, partly because there is increased competition from other countries and partly because current infrastructure is inadequate to support the world-wide trend towards increasing costs of science research (NCIHE, 1997; OST, 1997). There have been a variety of estimates for this shortfall and the Dearing Report suggested ways to address this: creating adequate cost and evaluation of resource use within research contracts, establishing a rolling fund for infrastructure and greater collaboration between institutions over facilities (NCIHE, 1997).

The government has to some extent acted upon these recommendations through the Competitiveness White Paper and Comprehensive Spending Review. Through these channels the government announced that, in partnership with the Wellcome Trust, it would spend an additional £1.4 billion on research in the 1999-2002 period. The aim of these additional resources is to modernise the UK science and engineering base and equip it for the next century.

While this extra spending will doubtless be of benefit as it filters through, the cracks it aims to fill are formidable and there is some indication from larger companies that they are increasingly siting their R&D abroad. Their reasons relate to a perceived drop in quality of research and graduates but also due to the increased competitiveness of foreign R&D. For example, ABPI noted, in their response to Dearing, that one leading member of their organisation placed 27 per cent of their academic research expertise outside the UK. In 1988 that figure was five per cent.

So how much interaction is actually going on?

In terms of the model in Figure 1.2 then, we need to look at interactions above the central arrow for evidence of cultural change and projects to develop 'mutual understanding'. We need to look at interactions below the arrow for evidence that the UK is becoming a high-growth innovation-based economy. Initial evidence is not that encouraging:

- SPRU research indicates that US industry collaborates in most disciplines with universities more than UK firms, except in chemistry and physics. However, the rate of increase of such interactions is faster in the UK. This suggests that, although the UK is doing fairly well in the level of interactions, more of this may be in contract and consultancy work than in collaborative research. The Innovation-Exploitation Barrier report (Select Committee on Science and Technology, 1997) also noted this increase in interactions but expressed concern that much of this was short-term work. The anecdotal evidence for this research would support these findings.

- Proportionately more academics are involved in running their own businesses and exploiting research via a start-up in the US relative to the UK (Scottish Enterprise, 1996).

- Research funding tends to be heavily concentrated in certain institutions and departments, often those that already do high quality basic and strategic research, suggesting the importance of high quality science in attracting applied work and more fundamental collaborations (Senker 1998). Universities that do not naturally attract this type of funding tend to focus on applied 'outreach' activities which fall outside the RAE formal assessment and, hence, funding remit.

This, and to some extent the data in Tables 1.2 and 1.3, gives rise then, to some fundamental concerns about the nature of university-industry collaborations. In particular, successive research highlights the difficulty in these collaborations which prevent the effective operation of the model, or system, which is given in Figure 2 (Scottish Enterprise, 1996; Senker 1998; POST 1997; Elliot, 1999; DTI 1998a). These are listed below:

- Difficulty in IPR negotiations.

- Lack of research ready for commercialisation (risks too high).

- Lack of development finance.

- Difficulties in interaction because of variations in attitudes to, for example, timescales.

- Barriers to 'access and absorption' (determined by differences in training and background of university and business employees and numbers of Qualified Scientists and Engineers (QSEs) in companies).

- R&D regarded as a specialist activity rather than one which should be integrated into boardroom discussions and strategy.

All this simply re-affirms the importance of the cultural issues in links and technology transfer between universities and industry discussed above. It is towards changing this culture that policy must be directed. Unless this cultural change can be effected the potential of British universities will remain unrealised.

Current policy to encourage and facilitate linkages between universities and industry

Overview

Prior to the Competitiveness White Paper, the last comprehensive policy statement on science policy came in the report *Realising our Potential* published by the last Conservative Government in 1993. It stated that the goals of the science base were to 'promote high quality basic, strategic and applied research, and related post-graduate training, thereby enhancing the United Kingdom's industrial competitiveness and quality of life'. This was a radical statement, bringing more focus to funding allocations and attempting to increase the proportion of research likely to be useful to industry. The Research Councils were restructured and encouraged to include greater involvement of users of research in their management and strategic allocation of funds.

These endeavours were further refined by the Technology Foresight exercise which reported in 1995 – an attempt to apply strategic and scenario planning to articulate the scientific needs of the future in order to underpin both quality of life and future industrial markets. Involving both scientists and industrialists, it was aimed at targeting resources on relevant broad research areas and creating strategic partnerships between academia and industry. The results of these exercises were used partially to direct Research Council and governmental department priorities for funding and to promote networks of business and academia. Subsequent analysis indicates that the exercise was very successful in creating these links (POST, 1997).

With the increase in the number of universities and the increasing costs of research, there is an on-going debate about how best to allocate the research budget between disciplines, institutions, departments and individuals. The Research Assessment Exercise has been used to target funding council research funds and the probable result of its continuation, together with Research Council priorities, is to lead to more concentration and selectivity of research money.

There has been no abatement in the interest devoted to industry-academia interactions. The Conservatives focused on trying to make the science base more 'relevant' whilst at the same time withdrawing support from more near market work. For example, the Advanced Technology Programme was withdrawn in favour of funding for more pre-competitive research initiatives such as LINK.

The Labour government's White Paper, *Our Competitive Future: Building the Knowledge Driven Economy*, places the commercial exploitation of knowledge from the science base at the centre of its vision of how the British economy should be modernised to meet the challenge of a high-tech future:

> A knowledge-driven economy is one in which the generation and exploitation of knowledge has come to play the predominant part in the creation of wealth. It is not simply about pushing back the frontiers of knowledge; it is also about the more effective use and exploitation of all types of knowledge in all manner of economic activity (DTI, 1998a).

Its approach both diverges from and builds upon the science policy developed by the Conservatives in the first half of the 1990s. Perhaps the most substantial divergence comes in the shift of resources toward the modernisation of research infrastructure in the science base, the aim of a large proportion of the additional £1.4 billion of spending to be carried out in partnership with the Wellcome Trust. Under the Conservatives, in contrast, it was widely felt that spending on infrastructure was inadequate to support the worldwide trend towards the increasing costs of science research (NCIHE, 1997).

Beyond this, however, the main thrust of the White Paper, as far as science policy is concerned, is to increase funding for existing programmes which are felt to have been successful, or have the potential to be so, such as the Teaching Company Scheme, Faraday Partnerships and Foresight Link – and to introduce some small-scale programmes which encourage university-industry interaction or commercialisation of knowledge from the science base. The new initiatives are along the right lines and a move toward creating an innovation policy and not just a science and technology policy, but are rather too piecemeal to bring about a dramatic change in the UK's innovation performance.

Technology transfer embodied in people

Technology transfer is about much more than just passing on knowledge. It requires that the firm is able to take up and exploit this information. As was noted earlier, this often requires that the company has the personnel and resources to do so. Successful technology transfer often necessitates the presence of qualified scientists and engineers (QSEs) who are able to interact with outside sources of information. Various schemes exist to encourage both technology transfer and to illustrate the benefits of employing trained researchers.

Teaching Company Scheme (TCS)

The TCS supports partnerships between companies and universities to help technology transfer and forge relationships. The TCS Directorate summarises the goals of the programme as:

- To facilitate the transfer of technology and the spread of technical and management skills, and to encourage industrial investment in training, research and development.

- To provide industry based training, supervised jointly by academic and industrial staff, for young graduates intending to pursue careers in industry.

- To enhance the levels of academic research and training relevant to business by stimulating collaborative research and development projects and forging lasting partnerships between academia and business.

Grants are given to universities to support the programmes which are undertaken by young graduates, TCS Associates, under joint supervision of company and academic staff for 1-3 years. The private sector puts up on average half the money but the percentage varies depending on whether the company is an SME or a large enterprise. A review of the scheme reported that for every one million pound grant spent it was believed that the programme produced 58 jobs, £3.6 million of value added, £3 million exports and £13.3 million turnover (TCS, 1997). TCS seemed to be successful in transferring technology to all sizes of firm. Of the firms surveyed, around three-quarters had introduced new or enhanced products or processes and there was a positive effect on profits, turnover, and employment. HEIs found a resultant increase in their links with industry.

As a result of TCS successes and of the apparent under-utilisation of the scheme, the Competitiveness White Paper proposed that the DTI's contribution be doubled. This would enable around 200 extra projects per year to be backed.

Co-operative Awards in Science and Engineering (CASE)

These awards are largely financed by the Research Councils with some industrial money and they support doctoral research on projects jointly devised and supervised by an academic department and a company. Industrial CASE is the same but the Research Councils allocate the awards to companies so that they can support projects at universities of their choice. There have been 896 awards overall with the majority coming from the EPSRC.

Postgraduate Training Partnerships (PTPs)

PTPs are a joint initiative of the DTI and the EPSRC. They involve partnerships between industry, RTOs and universities aimed at providing training for postgraduates and the transfer of skills and knowledge to industry. PTP Associates, high quality doctoral students with an interest in applying technology, are jointly supervised by the RTO and the university on commercial projects. They work at the RTO and also receive formal training in business skills such as presentation, project and time management. The overall costs of the PTP scheme have been around £2.8 million per year from the DTI to the RTOs while the EPSRC funds the associates via CASE awards.

RTOs are used as the intermediary since they can translate industry's needs and objectives into relevant and exploitable research. Companies benefit from accessing leading edge research and expertise in problem solving. Universities receive information about industry's needs in training and research and the partnership with the RTO provides a mechanism for technology transfer. The RTO benefits from the interactions both with universities and companies and is thus better able to play the role of intermediary. Students who pass through the scheme seem to have better employment prospects, tending to start on a higher salary.

Creating networks

The first section noted the importance of informal contacts and networks as a crucial part of the infrastructure for innovation. There are many examples of local initiatives and some Research Council and government department schemes aimed at increasing dialogue between companies and academics by providing fora and/or comprehensive information about expertise and services available.

Support for collaborative work

There is a variety of schemes and funding mechanisms supporting collaborative work of the type investigated by the case studies. One indirectly encourages collaboration by rewarding work already done with industry while another specifically targets collaborations. Further support comes from Research Council initiatives.

The rationale for policy initiatives and public funding are to encourage collaborations which would not have gone ahead without support and to cover the public sector input to the project. The current schemes tend to focus on pre-competitive research.

Realising Our Potential Awards (ROPAs)

These awards are run by the Research Councils and reward academics who have received finance from industry for basic or strategic research. The money has to be used to support speculative work of the academic's own choosing. The awards are also intended to encourage future collaboration opportunities between science and industry.

A survey of researcher attitudes to ROPA in January 1997 (DTI, 1997) concluded that the scheme had been successful in encouraging those researchers who had sought an award to seek more industry funding and new collaborations but had had little effect on those who had not looked for such finance. They noted that stronger drivers for industry collaborations were actually pressure on research funds and academics concerned about the relevance of their work. The survey suggested that the scheme may be more successful at extending collaboration between existing partners than in creating new ones.

LINK

LINK was launched in 1986 with the specific aim of bridging the gap between the science base and industry. It generally supports generic and strategic collaborative research between industry and academia rather than fundamental or development work. The research has to be of strategic importance to the economy. Each LINK programme consists of projects which last 1-5 years and involve one or more firms working with one or more science base partners (including HEIs and other public sector bodies). By 1997 there had been 57 LINK programmes. Funding is matched public and private finance, with the public money coming from Research Councils or Government departments.

Examples of programmes are Advanced and Hygienic Food Manufacture; Genetic and Environmental Interactions in Health; Inland Surface Transport. All partners contribute financial and other resources towards the achievement of those goals – including intellectual resources.

Recently support for Foresight projects has been included under the LINK banner. The DTI allocated £10 million in 1997 to Foresight LINK. This replaced the Foresight Challenge fund which was set up after Phase I of Technology Foresight to support projects aimed at taking forward priorities identified in the exercise. One example is a new National Centre for Applied Catalysis and a National Creative Technologies Initiative has been set up to underpin the creative industries (POST, 1998).

The perceived success of Foresight LINK in encouraging university-business links in areas thought to be of long-term strategic importance led to a further £10 million of DTI backing for a second round of Foresight LINK awards being announced in the CWP. A note of criticism has been sounded, however, by Senker (1998), who pointed out that small firms with QSEs may link up with HEIs informally but do not get involved in larger scale schemes of the type funded by this programme. Either they do not know that they exist or feel that the costs for participation and the length of the commitment are not possible given their available resources. She said that 'They perceive that these schemes had been designed to meet the needs of well-resourced large firms, with the time and personnel able to comprehend and fill in the long, complex forms and the financial resources to get involved in long term research projects.' This is particularly important since there is evidence that small innovative firms can benefit more from their links with universities than larger firms with their own R&D facilities (Feldman, 1994).

Research Council schemes

Research Councils have their own exploitation policies and strategic programmes which encourage collaboration between users and the science base. They fund formal collaborative projects and there is also more informal association with research funded by a third party (managed programmes). Potential users can thus gain early insights into both basic and more applied work. There is some low level input by the user involving the provision of small amounts of funding, materials, equipment, facilities or informal monitoring and mentoring of research.

Faraday Partnerships

The Faraday Partnerships initiative focuses on improving the interaction between the science base and industry, through the involvement of intermediate institutions. The idea of Faraday Partnerships was first mooted in the early 1990s and was to be a joint initiative between the EPSRC, the DTI and HEIs. Within government, it was deemed too expensive, however, and the idea was shelved until 1995-6 when the EPSRC decided to fund four Faraday Centres without help from the DTI. The particular role of the intermediate institutions is to develop a pattern of co-ordinated research with the science, engineering and technology base, which relates to the research requirements of an industrial sector and, in particular, the SME community within that sector.

The Partnerships aim to:

● increase the flow between universities and industry of research results, advanced technology and skilled scientists, engineers and technologists.

● increase the awareness in academia of industry's requirements for new technologies and skilled scientists and engineers.

● increase the exploitation within industry of research undertaken by the science and engineering base.

● develop and build on strong effective networks between academia and industry, especially SMEs.

The four Faraday Partnerships are:

● The East Midlands Faraday Partnership, PRIME, which serves the needs of the industry of systems builders providing complex hybrid electronic/mechanical products together with their supply chain of SMEs.

● The Intelligent Sensors for Control Technologies Partnership (INTErSECT) initiates new research and means for dissemination of information on intelligent sensing and measurement systems.

● The 3D Multimedia Applications and Technology Integration Centre (3D-MATIC) aims to help SMEs to gain access to new developments in automatic three-dimensional digitisation, which promises to revolutionise many design and analysis processes.

● The White Rose Partnership for Enhanced Packaging Technology forms a distributed centre of excellence in research and technology aligned to the needs of the packaging and related industries.

Each of the four Partnerships was given initial funding of up to £50,000 by the EPSRC and could then receive up to one million pounds subsequently for collaborative research projects and for education and training programmes.

The Competitiveness White Paper announced that the government plans a national network of Faraday Partnerships, with DTI support building on the initial work of the EPSRC. Funding for a second round of Faraday Partnerships was announced in September 1999, with the DTI contributing £4.8 million and the EPSRC £4 million for the creation of four more Partnerships. The eventual aim is to have 20 Faraday Partnerships in operation by early next century.

The Dearing Report and industry-academia interactions

The most recent debate over university interactions with industry was initiated by the National Committee of Inquiry into Higher Education, which produced its results in the Dearing Report (NCIHE, 1997). With reference to the range of programmes outlined above, Dearing stated that 'We have concerns – which have been echoed by many industrialists and academics – that such a large number of schemes is confusing' and argued further that 'there would be value in reviewing the extent to which these schemes provide a coherent framework for the promoting of research interactions'.

The question of whether the range of existing policy provision is adequate and whether gains could be made through greater rationalisation and coherence is explored in the analyses reported in Chapters 2 to 6, and especially in Chapter 7.

Concluding remarks

The chapter began with a discussion of a transfer model which illustrated the trajectory along which industry-academia interactions are currently developing. Two main features of the landscape currently prevent the effective operation of that model – cultural resistance to collaboration and creating entrepreneurial behaviour within universities. It was argued that there are plenty of 'partnership projects' between universities and industry which allow the cultural resistance to be broken down. However, the rationale behind enhancing university-industry links rests on the desire at a policy level to tap the latent innovative potential within universities and, accordingly, address the productivity gap, the perceived under-performance in UK product and process innovation and to create economic growth. Existing policies represent moves in the right direction – in particular the role of RDAs and Regional Innovation Strategies will be key in integrating universities into existing industrial structures. But only by addressing the issues of technology transfer, innovation and entrepreneurial behaviour will policy be able to achieve these objectives. This is necessarily complex and rests on the need to balance the misunderstandings about each other's activities with the desire to create real value added for both sides.

Endnotes

1   Evidence from 'participant observation' by the author.
2   Continuous Improvement for Competitive Advantage at the Centre for Research in Innovation Management, CENTRIM, University of Brighton.
3   Complex Product Systems: A joint university-industry research project run by SPRU and CENTRIM.
4   The arguments contained in this section relate to enhancing interactions in civilian R&D (ie non-defence R&D).

2. Pharmaceuticals and biotechnology

Introduction

The need for policy in co-ordinating, indeed systematising, the linkages between universities and industry is clear from the model developed in Chapter 1. The discussion there centred around two types of interaction, 'partnership' and 'business' programmes, and argued that the former represents means of developing mutual understanding of each other's values and beliefs while the latter represented a means of generating high-growth business opportunities and spin-outs. It is these latter types of collaboration, then, that may appear particularly suitable to the hi-tech and radically innovative structures represented by the pharmaceuticals and biotechnology sectors. Policy leverage for stimulating these sectors comes from tools such as equity and seedcorn funds and fiscal incentives for joint projects leading to the *creation* of small and medium-sized enterprises (SMEs) rather than innovations instigated by SMEs themselves.

The two sectors have been particularly successful in the UK, since both sectors spend vast amounts on research and development (R&D) and since university-industry partnerships are dominant features of the sectoral landscape. This chapter presents the main features of the two industries and explains why they are characterised by strong links with the public sector research (PSR) base. We then look in more detail at two examples of collaboration – the links developed by Glaxo Wellcome, with particular reference to the Edward Jenner Institute for Vaccine Research; and the Medical Research Council's collaborative work, with special focus being placed on its Collaborative Centre at Mill Hill. The research intensity of this sector means that some of the specific features are not transferable, however, there are lessons to be learned.

The pharmaceutical industry

Many early pharmaceutical products, such as Bayer's aspirin, were by-products of the chemical industry that was dominated by German and Swiss firms until World War Two. The post-war period saw the rise of the modern research-based industry, characterised by extensive patenting and a drug discovery process akin to molecular roulette in which thousands of chemical compounds were screened in the search for new chemical entities with identifiable therapeutic effects. In 1935, when the first modern anti-bacterial drug – Sulfonilamide – was introduced, May and Baker, its discoverers, had screened 693 compounds. By the 1960s, typically 8,000-10,000 compounds would be screened for every useful product launched (Sharp, 1991).

Today, although there is still much uncertainty and risk attached to drug discovery, the hit and miss nature of those early days has passed. Increasingly, drugs are being designed rather than discovered. They are being sought on the basis of a greater depth of understanding about the body's own biochemistry and immune system. Biotechnology, which has brought the cloning of the body's own therapeutic proteins, is now recognised as an essential part of this revolution and an increasing number of drugs are likely to derive from this route (Sharp and Patel, 1996).

Biotechnology

At its broadest, biotechnology involves the 'processing of biological agents', including micro-organisms, cultured cells and enzymes. As such, biotechnology has been practised since the earliest production of beer and wine (Faulkner and Senker, 1995). However, it was the development of genetic engineering techniques in the mid-1970s that brought the term 'biotechnology' into widespread usage and sparked interest in the field. The earliest genetic engineering included recombinant DNA techniques (invented at Stanford University in the US) by which genetic material is transferred from one organism to another, such that the 'host' produces proteins (and so performs reactions) which occur naturally in the 'donor'. *Hybridoma* techniques (invented at the Cambridge Laboratory of Molecular Biology in the UK) are used to fuse different cell types to produce monoclonal (meaning antigen specific) antibodies; by their very specificity, they enormously simplify and speed up the tasks of analysis and extraction.

Reasons for university-industry collaboration

While it is important not to exaggerate this (Anderson and Fears, 1995), Faulkner and Senker explain why the character of innovation in pharmaceuticals and biotechnology lends itself to links with PSR more readily than in other sectors:

> In the pharmaceutical industry innovation is probably closer to the classic 'linear model' than in any other sector. New product development is strongly knowledge-led, demanding heavy investment in well-equipped research laboratories; R&D is comparatively remote from both the user and production...in pharmaceuticals, R&D is particularly science-like and research-based... Together, these features explain why PSR linkage is stronger in pharmaceuticals companies than in other sectors. (Faulkner and Senker, 1995:192)

In addition, universities and their associated research underpin industry through the provision of trained researchers, new ideas and as a medium for the development of emerging technologies. Industrial association with academia often provides shape and direction to the research being undertaken. Expansion of the science base within universities through industrial funding allows insight into potentially novel biological and chemical targets. Much of the research in academia is of a fundamental nature and far removed from exploitation as a pharmaceutical product, but it is essential that this basic underlying science is undertaken if industrial scientists are to gain an understanding of, for example, the aetiology and cellular and molecular basis of certain diseases (Simpson, 1998).

The pharmaceutical industry employs a diverse range of scientific disciplines ranging from molecular modelling and genetics to large-scale engineering. It is not possible for industry to perform 'in-house' research on all developing technologies in each of these disciplines. Furthermore, no major pharmaceutical company can afford to lag too far behind its competitors in the race to develop a particular novel technology. Therefore, companies expand their portfolio of projects by pursuing collaborations with academic groups. For example, extensive networking by industrialists with academia may allow them to keep a watching brief on two or more competing technologies that ultimately may have the same aim. The technology that emerges as the front-runner may then be taken 'in-house' and further developed (Skingle, 1998).

Most collaborations between industry and academics involve pre-competitive research. The industrially sponsored academic projects are usually associated with an industrial target but are not normally central to the progression of that research. This slightly less focused outlook allows the laterally thinking academic to question established hypotheses and to provide new ideas and stimulation to the industrial projects. Similarly, the more focused industrial scientist may add more discipline to re-orientate or focus the academic programme of research. This 'meeting of the minds' with scientists having such contrasting outlooks on their research can often result in a synergistic effect (Skingle, 1998).

Finally, academics are often keen to collaborate with industry, not for the funding per se, but in order to gain access to equipment, resources or technology that would not otherwise be available in the academic environment.

GlaxoWellcome and the Edward Jenner Institute for Vaccine Research

GlaxoWellcome

Glaxo and Wellcome (GW) merged in 1995 to form the world's largest pharmaceutical company. Prior to the merger, both companies had a long tradition of collaborating with universities in areas of research of mutual interest to academic and industrial scientists. It is perhaps not surprising, therefore, that the recently formed company spends more money on research in UK universities than any other pharmaceutical company. In 1997, GW spent more than £10 million on research project grants and studentships with UK universities (Skingle, 1998).

One of GW's most interesting collaborations with academic science, however, occurs more indirectly through the Edward Jenner Institute for Vaccine Research.

Edward Jenner Institute for Vaccine Research

The Jenner Institute, a not-for-profit company, was founded in 1996 and is housed in purpose-built laboratories at Compton in Berkshire. It has the following mission:

- To carry out scientific research, of the highest international standards aimed at:

  - understanding the immune responses against infectious organisms or malignant cells;

  - applying new knowledge and technologies to develop effective means of inducing protective or therapeutic immunity in humans;

  - developing models of human disease for studies of novel vaccines or new formulations;

  - developing new formulations to allow delivery of antigens to the immune system for the induction of protective immunity;

  - encouraging and supporting science and technology activities in the UK that may lead to the discovery of new vaccines for human disease.

- To provide a centre of excellence for the training of workers in those fields of science and technology relevant to the activities and interests of the institute.

- To promote the public understanding of vaccination and the potential of immunisation for controlling infectious and other diseases.

It is funded by four institutions in an innovative public-private partnership, as shown in Table 2.1. It received an additional £6 million from GW in support of capital expenditure in that year, which forms part of a total spending commitment of £40 million which GW has pledged over a ten year period. The sponsors did not think that this mission could be delivered by one university or even a consortium, since the researchers would be prevented from concentrating exclusively on this brief by their other research and teaching responsibilities. Hence, a dedicated research centre was set up.

GW supplies three members of the Institute's Board of Directors, including the Chair, with the public sector partners getting one each. These Directors appointed Professor Peter Beverley as the Scientific Head of the Institute and had some input into its research programme, although this was devised largely by Professor Beverley himself. He

Table 2.1 The funding structure of the Jenner Institute (1998)

Funding source	Grants (as % of the total)
GlaxoWellcome (GW)	50%
Medical Research Council (MRC)	25%
Biotechnology and Biological Sciences Research Council (BBSRC)	17%
Department of Health (DoH)	8%
Total funding	**£2 million**

characterises it as primarily 'focused blue sky research'. The programme

> ...is designed to carry out the mission of the Institute through a twin track strategy. On the one hand, much of the work aims to attack fundamental problems in immunology which are relevant to all vaccines. These are long-term studies. Other programmes are aimed at more immediate development of vaccine candidates or immunotherapy. (Edward Jenner Institute for Vaccine Research, 1998:6).

Its staff has been recruited almost entirely from within academia, with leading researchers being responsible for particular elements of the research programme and receiving support from PhD or postdoctoral researchers. The Institute's staff remain a part of the academic networks to which they belonged when they worked at universities, which helps them to remain in touch with the latest developments in basic research.

Where the Institute's research leads to findings which may have the potential for commercial exploitation, GW has 'first refusal' on the intellectual property (IP), although a more likely scenario is that the Institute would keep the IP while GW would be licensed to develop the product. Given its start date in 1996 and the fact that its research projects are all 5-10 years in length, no products had been developed by late 1999. Given the profitability of new pharmaceutical products, however, if even one were developed as a result of the Institute's research in the ten-year period to which GW is financially committed, this would represent a handsome return on the company's investment.

Medium-term product development is not, however, the primary reason why GW provides the bulk of the Jenner Institute's funding. As was noted earlier, it is not possible for a pharmaceutical company, even one as large as GW, to perform 'in-house' research on all developing technologies in each of the many disciplines in which it is involved. The areas of research on which the Jenner Institute concentrates are ones that GW believes are potential sources of new products in the long-term but where it has little in-house expertise at the present time. Also, the projected time-lag between the fundamental research and the development of new products is too long for GW's board to sanction a large amount of in-house research spending, which would of course not attract the extra funding provided by the public sector partners. By part funding the Institute, GW is covering the possibility that new product development possibilities may appear in the areas of vaccine research in which it specialises, without having to bear all of the costs or divert any of its in-house staff from the more development-oriented work in which, in any case, they tend to specialise.

Somewhat more controversially, it could also be argued that pharmaceutical company R&D departments are less proficient at blue sky research, albeit focused, than research institutes like Jenner. The concentration on high throughput screening or product development, often involving the improvement of drugs developed originally by other companies, does not provide a culture conducive to the more detached and reflective environment required for basic research. A comparison can also be drawn between the research carried out at Jenner and that by a small, leading edge biotechnology company, which will often be bought up by large pharmaceutical companies like GW once they have completed the 'research' stage of a project but are unable to successfully manage the 'development' (Simpson, 1998).

The incentives for the public sector partners to fund the Institute are somewhat different. The MRC has been criticised in the past for generating important scientific discoveries in its research centres but then not developing the products based upon them. By collaborating with GW in a venture such as this, they are maximising the chances of funding basic research that leads eventually to new product development, since GW has renowned expertise in near-market development work. It is GW researchers who have the primary role as 'translators' in this arrangement, with members of GW's Office of Scientific and Educational Affairs and its Research and Development department being members of the Jenner Board. They are well placed to identify those aspects of the Institute's research which are most likely to yield future products, as are the researchers from GW's Medicines Research Centre, its primary R&D facility in the UK, who work closely with the Jenner Institute researchers on a number of projects (interview notes). Even if the MRC is not ultimately responsible for taking the products to market, therefore, it would have contributed to a process by which a leading UK company has been able to do so. The same motivation applies to the BBSRC in a less pronounced way. The DoH's involvement is demand rather than supply driven: as the leading customer of the UK pharmaceutical industry, they have a vested interest in the development of improved products.

MRC Collaborative Centre

The MRC Collaborative Centre is a not-for-profit technology transfer organisation set up by the Medical Research Council in 1986 and located at Mill Hill in North London. It is on its own site adjacent to the National Institute for Medical Research, MRC's largest wholly funded research establishment, with which it has a number of links. In contrast to the Jenner Institute, the Centre's role is one of development rather than research: its main objective is to produce new medical treatments by exploiting MRC-funded research through project-based collaborations with industry. Over the past ten years, the Centre has become an international focus of technology transfer from MRC-funded research to the pharmaceutical and biotechnology industry.

The centre is self-financing and has been since 1993. It has received no direct financial support from MRC beyond an initial capital injection of £2.9 million which supported the initial five year plan between 1987 and 1992, and a 60-year lease at a peppercorn rent on its land. The centre employs some fifty people, around forty of whom are scientific researchers, and also plays host to visiting company scientists, up to ten of whom are based at the Centre at any one time. Over the past five years, an average of ten projects have been ongoing for around seven industry partners, while income has averaged three to four million pounds per annum. In the past three years, the Centre has also acted as incubator for Prolifix Ltd, a start-up company based on MRC discoveries in the cell area, and played a key role in its inception.

The focus of the MRC Collaborative Centre over the past ten years

---

Box 2.1 Prolifix

Prolifix, based in Abingdon, Oxfordshire, is a privately-held biotechnology company that was founded at the MRC Collaborative Centre, Mill Hill, in 1994. The company is based on the recognition that the discoveries being made on the cell cycle offered the prospect of significant new drug discovery targets, with potential applications in cancer and diseases of cellular proliferation. Prolifix's technology is based on its understanding of the processes that regulate growth and reproduction of cells – molecular processes that are widely seen as key to the discovery of new classes of drugs to alleviate disease. The company has secured a portfolio of intellectual property in this area and has built a series of proprietary drug discovery programmes. In June 1997, Prolifix raised £5.4 million in a second-round private placement led by Atlas Venture. Other investors include 3i plc, GIMV, the MRC, and Chugai Pharmaceuticals of Japan (with which Prolifix has a research collaboration).

---

has been on applied research on the following grounds:

- Commercial research is fundamentally different to academic research.

- Work to develop and exploit the results of academic research should take place in a dedicated but distinct environment.

- There is a need to prevent the MRC's basic research programme from being distorted by commercial objectives.

Projects developed to date have embraced a wide spectrum of life sciences research directed at drug discovery including: immunology; molecular genetics and molecular biology; molecular pharmacology; virology; neurobiology; antibody engineering; and vascular smooth muscle research. The Centre has also hosted a number of projects funded by the MRC in strategic areas, in particular the MRC AIDS Directed Programme (ADP). Box 2.2 contains more detailed information on a collaborative venture in which the Centre has recently been involved.

Projects are generally based on novel science undertaken at an MRC research establishment that has the potential for industrial application. In most cases, MRC will have filed patent applications on the basic technology and at least some initial development work will have been carried out by the Centre. This is then taken further through collaboration with industrial partners, which in the recent past have included companies such as Athena, Neurosciences, Chugai

---

Box 2.2 Oncogene Science Inc

The MRCCC and Oncogene Science Inc (OSI, Uniondale, NY, US) established a joint antiviral program which offers a new approach to the discovery of antiviral therapeutic agents. The program targets the essential viral proteins of human immunodeficiency virus (HIV), herpes simplex (HSV) and human hepatitis B (HBV). The collaboration focused initially on the viral proteins, Tat, Rev and Nef of HIV; ICP4 of HSV; and the reverse transcriptase of HBV. Currently, attention is directed to targets for hepatitis C and influenza. Oncogene Science has developed a proprietary cell based, ultra-high throughput automated screening technology, which extends the proven potential of random screening. This technology facilitates the cost-effective, rapid, and highly accurate testing of hundreds of thousands of test samples, enabling the identification of the best possible leads available within any chemical file. Each system can carry out up to 125,000 assays per week and in a year the total screening centre at Oncogene will evaluate over three million compounds. Also available to this particular collaboration is one of the world's largest fungal collections, corresponding to over 300,000 screening samples, coupled to an experienced in-house natural products chemistry group.

Pharmaceuticals, Ciba Geigy, E Merck, Glaxo Wellcome and the Marion Merrell Dow Research Institute.

The collaborative projects based at the Centre differ in several key respects from industry sponsorship of research at universities or in MRC units. The main distinction is that the projects being carried out at the Centre are viewed by the industry partners more as an extension of their in-house corporate research than as one of their sponsored academic collaborations, where the interaction is with independently motivated research. This distinction is reinforced by the technology transfer function of the Centre, through which company scientists join, and are trained alongside, the Centre team in order to successfully integrate and transfer the work into their in-house corporate research activity. The MRCCC acts as an intermediate institution, helping to 'translate' the findings of basic or academic research into near-market applications. Key players in this 'translator' role include senior MRC staff scientists, who either visit regularly or are seconded to the Centre for the duration of a project; and the MRCCC's Director, who is invariably a scientist of similar calibre to a research director of a biotechnology company.

Project management practices closely resemble those to be found in company R&D departments. In most cases the Centre takes direct responsibility for the day-to-day management of projects, setting objectives, monitoring progress and producing regular reports. Project management takes place in close co-ordination with industry partners within a commercially sensitive *extra mural* corporate research environment. The Centre negotiates licence options to MRC patents in connection with research collaborations. Companies are granted exclusive rights to work carried out by the Centre within specified fields of application. Where a licensing agreement is concluded, product royalties are paid to the MRCCC and are often very substantial, enabling the Centre to be self-financing. In this respect, the Centre can be seen to operate in a similar way to a biotechnology company, developing products to the stage where they can be patented but then licensing them to larger pharmaceutical companies who carry out further product development.

Conclusion – what can other sectors learn from these collaborations?

General

As stated at the outset, the pharmaceuticals and biotechnology sectors are particularly suited to 'business' type collaborations in technology transfer between academia and industry. Competitiveness in these sectors is dependent on innovation and, hence R&D spend and patenting. The fact that Glaxo Wellcome spends 80 per cent as much on research and development as it does on manufacture and supply underlines the degree to which its products are research-intensive, with very little improvement being possible through the production process once the product has been designed. It is because of these features that GW is willing, along with its public sector partners, to finance the speculative research carried out by the Jenner Institute and why so many pharmaceutical companies have been keen to collaborate with the MRCCC, so as to access research findings from the MRC science base.

The fact that these features are not present to the same extent in any other industry restricts the degree to which PSR-industry links in pharmaceuticals and biotechnology can be seen as 'blueprints' for other sectors. Nevertheless, it is possible to draw some conclusions from the Jenner and MRCCC case studies about the ingredients for successful university-industry collaboration.

Policy lessons

There are, then, a number of policy lessons that can be extracted from the discussion contained in this chapter:

- Particularly in hi-tech, but in other areas as well, the importance of risk spreading through partnership funding cannot be over-stated. Since the research conducted by universities is, by nature, 'blue sky', it is necessarily unpredictable in terms of its commercial potential. Projects may take years to build up commercial momentum, if, indeed, they ever do. But through partnership funding structures (evident in particular in the Jenner Institute), a critical mass of research develops from which the chances of commercial exploitation are maximised.

- Collaborative research should focus on the core interests of the academic scientists in the first instance since this guarantees the innovative quality of the output, but the end objective of commercialisation should not be forgotten. At the Jenner Institute, this trade-off is effected through the participation of industrial scientists in research projects, thereby ensuring that any commercial potential is identified.

- Similarly, participation of industrial scientists in research ensures that the 'translator role' is not lost – in other words, there are appropriate qualified personnel to carry the research results back into their industrial application.

- Projects in both cases are managed professionally – ie as they would be in a dedicated industrial R&D laboratory.

These measures allow the cultural gaps identified in Chapter 1 to be bridged while maintaining the naturally long term and blue sky perspectives of the academic partners. Any policies aimed at increasing the numbers of projects operating through similar 'business' partnerships have to take these cultural requirements into account.

3. Engineering and materials

It has already been suggested that the high-growth business type partnerships may be more appropriate to hi-tech than to more traditional sectors. This is not because knowledge is less important in these sectors, but rather because 'blue sky' research is not a means of creating competitive advantage. Hence, the role for university scientists is, perhaps less obvious. Further, these industries tend to have larger numbers of SMEs for whom the risk of partnerships with universities is disproportionate to the potential long-term gain.

And yet arguably it is in manufacturing and engineering that key weaknesses in UK productivity, product and process innovation and even growth are to be found. If the Government is to achieve its policy objectives in these areas, then, it must find mechanisms for stimulating these sectors, not least because they still account for a sizeable proportion of UK exports, employment and GDP (Technology Foresight Group 1995).

It is therefore worth exploring the transferability of the generic elements of existing partnerships in the pharmaceuticals and biotechnology structures and learning from existing best practice. Collaborative projects take two forms, as has already been shown: partnership (mutual understanding) – type programmes and 'business programmes' which lead to innovation and growth. The key elements in either type of project from the discussion so far are that they must contain all of the following elements:

- Management structures along commercial principles.

- Clear delineation between the 'research' and the 'commercial' elements of any projects.

- Critical mass of research.

- Effective 'translators' allowing the results of any project to be transferred into an industrial context with ease.

As was made clear from the hi-tech examples in the previous chapter, all of these elements can be 'embodied' in the personnel working within partnership research. It is necessary but not sufficient for companies to provide funding – they must also participate actively in the management, running and dissemination of the research. This is a remarkably 'low-tech', common sense solution that should be readily transferable into other industrial contexts. It is to this, then, that the discussion now turns through case studies of the Warwick Manufacturing Group (WMG) and the Sheffield Materials Forum (SMF).

Warwick Manufacturing Group

Professor Kumar Bhattacharyya set up WMG in 1980 with a base in the University of Warwick's Engineering department. University-industry interaction was unfashionable at the time, with both sides needing a lot of convincing that collaboration was worthwhile. Industrialists tended to see universities as 'charities' which did not understand business realities while, according to Bhattacharyya, firms had little idea how to access the intellectual capacity which resided in university science, engineering and technology departments.

His intention was to encourage links between companies and university engineers that would tackle the primary weakness of British engineering, which in his view was the poor quality of the product base. In the early 1980s, however, very few firms could be persuaded of the need for product development and so Bhattacharyya concentrated instead on trying to improve their skill base, in relation to which firms were more willing to admit there was a problem. He developed a club of about 30 companies, most of which were based in the West Midlands, and encouraged them to send him graduates for post-experience education programmes. In contrast to the 'generalist' courses prevalent in business schools, these programmes provided management training grounded in the engineering context. Groups of Warwick staff were simultaneously attached to companies to support the graduates and help them to apply their knowledge effectively in the business environment. Member companies eventually started to supply staff members as visiting lecturers at WMG as trust began to develop between the university and the firms. These courses, which were the forerunners of the current Integrated Graduate Development Scheme, led eventually to the building up of a stock of managers in engineering firms who were responsive to the need for enhancements in the product base. Their presence thus made it feasible for research collaboration between WMG and the regional manufacturing base to occur.

In 1995 WMG was Europe's biggest postgraduate centre for engineering R&D. Table 3.1 presents some summary data on the activities of WMG in 1998.

Table 3.1 Key data for Warwick Manufacturing Group	
Numbers of staff	474
Partnerships	300 companies (including R&D, technology transfer and post-experience education)
Numbers of students	Full time MSc = 400 Part time MSc = 800 >2,000 participants on Diplomas, Certificates, short courses (eg CAD training)
Number of courses	80
International activity	Teaching provision in Hong Kong, mainland China, Malaysia, Thailand, India, South Africa
Key partnerships	Rover (1985) founding partner in Advanced Technology Centre – led to partnerships with 40 other companies and development of K Series engine.
Research income	1999: £81.5 million
Source: Warwick Network 1998; SL interviews 1999	

Structure and organisation

The Group does not have a rigid hierarchical structure. It is organised around a group of semi-autonomous collaborative centres, each of which is managed by a senior researcher, reporting directly to Bhattacharyya. There is no management team. The centres include the CAD/CAM centre, the Computer Integrated Manufacturing facility, the Best Practice Unit and the Manufacturing Simulation team.

Within this framework, WMG carries out research of several different types. Contract and collaborative research carried out directly for large private sector firms is usually charged at commercial rates. The Group has a lot of discretion over what they can do with money obtained through this source. The position is similar with income produced through work with SMEs, except that in these cases the work is often carried out at a subsidised rate. With work financed by research councils or government departments, more conventional university rates are charged and the income has a smaller 'discretionary' component. In all cases, however, the university receives a substantial proportion of the revenue, which is then distributed among other departments.

Warwick University is highly supportive of industry collaboration. This is reflected in the 'industrially relevant salaries' (*The Economist*, 1995) which are paid to many WMG staff members in order to provide an incentive structure which encourages them to work effectively with industry. This reflects the fact that a great deal of collaborative work often mitigates against the more typical university career building based upon the accumulation of academic publications.

SMEs and the regional economy: education and technology transfer

WMG has worked with a considerable number of small and medium-sized enterprises (SMEs) as part of its collaboration with industry. Much of this work has been developed through its Manufacturing Excellence Initiative (MEI), an educational programme for SME managers and engineers which consists of 80 modules on a range of business, operational and technology topics. These modules, which can be accessed as a stand-alone course or as part of a mini programme across the management team, are designed to bring the essential components of business improvement within reach of the smaller company. They are often accessed by SMEs through 'industrial clubs' – forums of companies organised by local development agencies and universities that can leverage part funding for SME participation through local, national and European programmes. One such example of an industrial club was that brought together by Coventry City Council as part of its 'Going for World Class' initiative, in which Warwick and other West Midlands universities were involved. Two examples serve to highlight the emphasis placed on local SMEs.

Burbidge

Located only a mile from the University campus, Burbidge is a long-established family firm manufacturing kitchen doors and employing just over 100 people in 1995. Table 3.2 illustrates the case.

According to Burbidge, the technical assistance and advice provided by WMG was overwhelmingly the major factor in explaining their

Table 3.2 WMG case: Burbidge

The problem	1995 customer survey suggesting that priority should be given to improving delivery speed. Target: majority of deliveries within a week of order (currently 80% within two weeks).
The solution (initiated through 'Going for World Class' network and Warwick Manufacturing Simulation team)	Reorganisation of production process through computer simulation to shorten delivery times cost efficiently
The implementation	*Cost:* £5000
	Issues: sceptical management (cost seen as too high but matched funding came from Coventry City Council).
	Simulation results: re-organisation on Cell manufacturing principles; simplification of throughput; reduction in size of transfer batches; implementation of teamworking techniques.
	Networking activities: management visited other companies from 'Going for World Class Group' – learning opportunities
	Results: by 1997, 97% of doors delivered within a week; inventories down 40%, sales turnover up from £6m (1995) to £9m (1997)

improved performance. There are other important factors however, which need to be identified.

- First, even before its contact with WMG, the company had a more strategic orientation than is found in most SMEs. The very fact that they commissioned a customer survey to investigate how they might improve, in a non-crisis situation, is evidence of this. Quite a lot of the credit for this must rest with the Finance Director, who made the initial contact with WMG and, once the collaboration had started, acted as a 'translator' between WMG and the Manufacturing Director, who was initially unconvinced about the value of the arrangement. This can perhaps be explained by the fact that the Finance Director was one of only a small number of graduates employed by the firm and that, although trained as an accountant, he has a background in computing.

- Second, the 'Going for World Class' group played a 'networking' role in providing the forum through which SMEs interested in process development and universities interested in interaction could meet. Furthermore, the group's ability to subsidise WMG's involvement in the collaboration played a surprisingly important role in making it happen, given the relatively small sums of money involved, even for a firm of Burbidge's size. This shows both the importance of local networking frameworks and the potentially large impact of publicly funded support in this area.

- Third, the collaboration shows the benefits to be gained from a flexible charging structure on the part of universities. While WMG charges commercial rates when working with large firms, this work was probably carried out at a small loss. In the long term, however, by helping to improve the economic performance and technological capability of local SMEs, the group is building up its future client base in much the same way as it did through education programmes for managers in larger companies during the 1980s. This practice of sensitive pricing, when combined with a willingness on the part of university staff to answer day-to-day queries on the part of the firm without any additional charging, goes some way towards explaining how the university was able to build up a relationship of trust with the SME. It is this trust and confidence that explains why SMEs can be willing to contract universities to carry out what is fairly basic technology transfer work, which *a priori* might be considered more suitable for a research and technology organisation (RTO). The latter find it difficult to overcome the poor reputation of consultants in the eyes of many small companies.

Lanemark

A manufacturing SME located in the West Midlands. It employed 16 people at the time of its first contact with WMG, towards the end of 1993. Started in 1981 as a management buyout from Dunlop, it specialised during the 1980s and by the end of that decade had narrowed to its current focus on the design and manufacture of industrial heating systems. By 1990 its annual turnover had reached £1m.

Table 3.3 WMG case: Lanemark

The problem	1990-93 decline in annual turnover to £0.75m – almost bankrupt. *Target:* to double company turnover within a 2-3 year period.
The solution (initiated through Manufacturing Excellence Initiative, module attendance and successive meetings)	Focus on 'core' of industrial heating systems. Patents held in this area.
The implementation	*Issues:* lack of technical knowledge
	Solutions: attendance on MSc engineering courses; regular feedback meetings
	Results: by 1998, turnover of £3m; 28 employees; employed personnel from WMG's teaching company scheme (thus allowing R&D to be conducted). Increased exports to US and Japanese markets.

Table 3.3 shows the key aspects of this case.

As with Burbidge, there were a number of factors that helped them to make the link with WMG successful.

- First, although not initially well disposed towards the idea that a university could help him to improve his business, the MD did start from a position where he wanted to plan improvement over the medium-term rather than deal with short-term issues. This predisposition towards strategic thinking is to some extent a prerequisite for effective university-industry interaction. Whereas in the case of Burbidge it seemed to derive from the background of the Finance Director, in the case of Lanemark it probably came from the MD's prior experience in a large company, in which a culture of strategic planning would have been more common.

- Second, the provision of relatively small amounts of matched funding from the ERDF played an important role in enabling the collaboration to go ahead. Given the uncertainty that most SMEs feel about the likely benefits from interaction with universities, almost any amount of subsidisation will provide a 'comfort zone' that will stimulate knowledge links.

- Third, trust was again mentioned as an important factor in explaining why the collaboration was a success. The reluctance of WMG staff to commercially exploit the relationship had a favourable impact on Lanemark's Managing Director and partly explains why he remains in regular contact with the WMG staff with whom he worked.

Supply chains and product development

Bhattacharyya's primary criticism of British manufacturing is for the weakness of its product base. As such, one of the main objectives of WMG is to develop collaborative research projects that lead to improvements in product development. Due to the integrated nature of modern manufacturing processes, this also often involves interacting with the supply chains of the companies concerned.

Electromagnetic Compatibility (EMC) testing

The EMC Group, based in the Advanced Technology Centre (ATC), has carried out a number of collaborative research projects with Rover and its suppliers to develop new methods of testing whether in-car electronics operate as intended, even in the face of severe radio frequency (RF) interference. This is an important area of research because electronics are applied widely in modern cars and control critical functions such as the engine and brakes, as well as less vital comfort and entertainment features.

Traditionally, EMC testing is carried out in large chambers, built at great expense. The screened chamber, which contains an antenna and the vehicle to be tested, is coated internally with a radio frequency absorbent layer to cut down reflections. In the test a vehicle is run, without a driver, on a rolling road while the operation of the many vehicle systems is monitored from the safety of the control room through instrumentation and closed-circuit TV. The interference signal for the test is produced by an RF signal generator and amplified to the level necessary to produce the required field strength (Ball, Jennings and Lever, 1992).

In addition to the cost, a further problem with this procedure is that it occurs at a relatively late stage of the vehicle development process, as indicated by Figure 3.1 below.

Figure 3.1

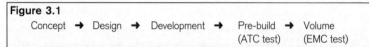

Concept → Design → Development → Pre-build → Volume
                                  (ATC test)   (EMC test)

As a prototype vehicle is required to do the testing, it cannot be carried out until the pre-build stage. Clearly, if any development work is needed at this stage for the electrical systems to pass the test, engineers are under great pressure to finish the work quickly because of the expense of using the facility and the late stage at which the test occurs in the vehicle development process.

WMG began collaborative work with Rover in the early 1990s to substantially reduce the cost of the EMC testing procedure and to bring it forward to the 'development' stage of the process (see Figure 3.1). The aim was to devise a means of pretesting electronic systems away from the vehicle, so that any necessary development could be carried out by the supplier company well in advance of the whole vehicle test – which would remain as a 'sign-off' formality (Ball, Jennings and Lever, 1992). Unfortunately, however, the electromagnetic behaviour of a component when operated on a bench top is quite different from its behaviour when installed in a vehicle. So the new test had to have two parts: a bench-top test procedure and a 'transfer function' to convert the results into those that would be seen in the vehicle.

The bench-top test procedure adapted a process already used in the aerospace industry (Carter, 1982). This involved the 'bulk current injection' (BCI) technique, where the interfering signal is introduced into the component via its connecting wires. The Warwick work was able to calculate the statistical likelihood of the vehicle passing the test, given the results of the BCI procedure and the characteristics of the vehicle. By making use of a large database on the results of previous tests, it was able to do this with a high degree of statistical reliability. This statistical information was then written into the software that drives the BCI equipment, to give a test procedure that is easy to run and can be applied at a relatively early stage of the product development process. It came quickly into routine use at Rover.

To implement this test for suppliers, a Rover Engineering Standard was issued which required that a BCI susceptibility profile be produced for each new component. Initially, the analysis was carried out by Rover's research engineers to allow suppliers to become familiar with BCI techniques, but after a training programme the engineers in supplier companies were able to perform the work. The significance of this research project is as follows:

- By enabling EMC testing to occur at an earlier stage of the product development process, it reduced the costs associated with rectifying those electronic systems that failed the test.

- By extending the test to components, it made testing of the pre-build vehicle a formality, so that time-consuming adjustments to the prototype were no longer required, at least for the purposes of rectifying electronic system faults. This speeded up the product development process and reduced time to market.

- The research had considerable academic kudos and was published in a number of academic journals.

The project also provided the foundation for a further piece of collaborative research between WMG and Rover, which started in September 1997 and is ongoing. This is the Wiring Harnesses: Electromagnetic Effects of Lightweight Structures (Wheels) project, funded as part of the Innovative Manufacturing Initiative (IMI). This is a programme funded by the EPSRC, BBSRC and ESRC (Economic and Social Research Council), that requires matching funding from the industrial partners, which in this case includes a number of Rover suppliers and a software company, as well as Rover itself. The aim of this project is to push the EMC testing further back into the product development process, to the 'design' rather than the 'development' stage. If this were successful, it would bring further reductions in both costs and lead times.

Intermediate institutions – facilitator and translator

Two examples highlight the importance of the facilitator and translator role in university-industry links as they are practised in the WMG.

Rapid Prototyping and Tooling (RP&T)

A technique for generating real solid models of components, directly from 3D computer-assisted design (CAD) models, in a matter of hours. This results in increased speed, ability to utilise complex product systems (CoPS – ie components and multiple modules and clients), repeatable accuracy and direct use of CAD data.

RP&T machines were first developed in the US in 1989 and Rover bought the first one to appear in the UK in 1992. After seeing it in operation, WMG researchers soon realised its wide scope for application, bought their own machine and devoted resources to developing the technology. At the same time, Rover took steps to encourage their suppliers to start using the technology: both the Rover and WMG machines were hired out to Rover suppliers and WMG carried out the necessary training of their engineers.

This work with Rover's supply chain led to an increase in awareness of RP&T, both in the West Midlands and beyond. WMG started to receive calls from companies wishing to hire the machine and organised daily tours to educate local businesses about the benefits of RP&T. A dedicated member of staff was employed to deal with RP&T enquiries and this led to the establishment of an RP&T club with its own newsletter, 'Rapid News'. The club eventually attracted financial assistance from the European Regional Development Fund, although in truth its membership was national and increased quickly to about 250 companies, each of which paid an annual subscription. The club became too large to manage within WMG and so formed its own trade association, the Rapid Prototyping and Manufacturing Association (RPMA), which in 1997 became part of the Institution of Mechanical Engineers.

Rover Advanced Power Train Technology Laboratory (RAPTTL)

Rover Group's Advanced Power Train Technology Laboratory (RAPTTL) was relocated to WMG's Advanced Technology Centre in 1993, having previously been located at the nearby Gaydon Test Centre, one of Rover's primary R&D facilities. RAPTTL is part of Rover's R&D department and carries out basic research on engine development. The Laboratory employs about 25 staff, who jointly supervise PhD students from Warwick and are involved in regular collaboration with about 30 Warwick staff at any point in time. In addition, collaborative research is conducted with engineers from several other universities, especially Leeds, Cambridge, Oxford, Loughborough, Brunel and Imperial.

Perhaps the most interesting aspect of the RAPTTL from the viewpoint of university-industry links is that it has very little contact with WMG researchers. Of the 30 Warwick staff with whom it has regular links, only about two or three are from the Manufacturing

Group – the majority are more theoretical researchers from other parts of the Engineering Department and other departments altogether, such as Physics and Mathematics. Its location within the Advanced Technology Centre, however, which is part of the WMG site, *facilitates* its links with non-WMG researchers. There is a concentration of theoretical expertise in Warwick's science and engineering departments that can be accessed due to the Laboratory's location within the Manufacturing Group. This also gives the RAPTTL access to some high quality PhD students, many of whom are recruited by the company after finishing their theses. Being located in the West Midlands is also advantageous for the Laboratory, because it is close to the Gaydon Test Centre near Coventry and Rover's Longbridge plant in Birmingham.

Education and training

WMG now provides a wide range of post-experience education courses, ranging from short and bespoke courses for industry to the Engineering Doctorate (EngD). The key feature of all these courses, which tends to set them apart from most university teaching provision, is that the academic-industrial partnership sets the objectives, determines content, jointly delivers the material, regularly reviews and updates it, and assesses participants through in-company project work. The aim of this is to develop programmes that combine academic excellence with industrial relevance. They aim to develop executives and managers who can successfully handle the complexities of an engineering business. The various schemes are built from a portfolio of over 80 courses, which blend personal and vocational development in business skills, technological understanding and managerial capability. They are structured to provide flexibility in entry and exit points, as illustrated in the case boxes which follow.

Box 3.1   The Engineering Doctorate (EngD)

The Engineering Doctorate aims to develop individuals who cannot only innovate but who can also implement that innovation. It is a research degree of an equivalent level to the PhD but with very different objectives – in particular, innovation in the application of knowledge rather than simply a contribution to the body of knowledge. It is highly flexible and able to accommodate participants at all levels of a company up to and including board level. WMG is one of five centres chosen by the Engineering and Physical Sciences Research Council to pilot this new degree. It has grown to be the biggest of the centres, with over one hundred participants now registered on the programme supported by over 30 different companies including Lucas, Rover Group, Raychem, Rolls Royce, Ricardo and 3M.

Box 3.2 Bachelor of Engineering (BEng)

WMG is pioneering a new approach to undergraduate training in partnership with Rover Group. This innovative degree course moves students from the lecture theatre to the shop floor. About 75 per cent of the degree consists of carefully planned work assignments in which the students put their academic studies into practice. People already working in manufacturing, through a combination of academic study and development of work based competencies, work towards a B.Eng. in Technology and Business Management. Students spend two days a week in the classroom and the remaining three in the business and work-based credits are assessed by the business. Initially students are given academic training at a College of Further Education and later progress to Warwick University where they take courses alongside full time BEng. undergraduates. The first Partnership Degree students graduated in 1996 and in 1997 a further 12 followed. Next year the scheme will expand with BMW also taking UK engineering apprentices.

Box 3.3 Short courses for industry

Specialist courses of interest to industry are offered in a range of subjects. Many dedicated courses and course programmes are tailored for individual company (for example, the Commercial Purchasing Programme for BAe). Requirements range from the basic Integrated Engineering Business Management material such as Project Management, Quality Management, Logistics, Rapid Prototyping to the Design of Manufacturing Systems. Several short courses are available in various aspects of microcomputer principles and applications. Extensive practical experience in the Engineering laboratories forms an essential feature of these. A number of short courses in Civil and Mechanical Engineering are available from time to time and a new series of courses in Nanotechnology began in 1992.

Interim remarks

It was noted at the beginning of this section that WMG's scale of operation and, to a certain extent, its maturity, set it apart from most university-based organisations that boast extensive interactions with industry. It operates largely as an intermediate research organisation, perhaps more akin to the Fraunhofer structures discussed in more detail in Chapter 6 than to the 'spin-out' university-industry type projects which perhaps operate in hi-tech 'below the line' of technology transfer identified in the model of Chapter 1. The examples discussed above provide further illustration of the success it has achieved by performing productive partnerships with the business sector.

Sheffield Materials Forum

Overview

The Sheffield Materials Forum (SMF) was established in 1993 as an association of large local companies who had a common interest in engineering materials and the University of Sheffield. Its intention was to build on the region's long-standing manufacturing and research strengths in materials science and engineering. While the scale of SMF's operation has not reached anything like the levels of WMG, this is partly deliberate and reflects differences in objectives and orientation.

The Forum was very much a 'top down initiative', conceived by Sheffield's vice-chancellor, Professor Sir Gareth Roberts, as a way of strengthening links between the university and local industry. His motivation was partly to develop university-industry connections where they were much weaker than should be the case, but also to stimulate inter-firm linkages which had been an important feature of Sheffield's industrial past but had waned considerably during the de-industrialisation of the 1970s and 1980s.

While Roberts had good relationships with local business leaders, he did not quite have the credibility to overcome the marked scepticism which most of them felt about the benefits to be gained from closer links with the university. To this end, he persuaded a prominent local businessman, Doug Liversidge, to get involved in the project and 'sell it' to the business community. Liversidge set out to do this along with Marilyn Wedgwood of the university's Regional Office, who similarly sought to encourage researchers from the university's highly rated engineering departments to collaborate more closely with firms in the context of the Forum's activities.

As well as lending credibility to the Forum in the eyes of major engineering firms in the region, Liversidge was also able to ensure that contact was made in the first instance with the managing director or chief executive, rather than the research and development director. This was seen as important because links with universities can often become marginal to the firm if senior management is not involved from the outset. Despite this personal connection, persuading firms to get involved and pay the annual subscription was difficult. This was despite the fact that the cost was only set at £3,000 and only one of the companies approached was an SME.

Within a year however, eleven firms had joined SMF. These were all companies with at least one major plant in the local region that had a strong interest in metals and engineering materials processing or related industries. Within the University, researchers from the Department of Engineering Materials were, and remain, most heavily involved in the Forum, but the Departments of Mechanical Engineering and Automatic Control and Systems Engineering are also represented. The Materials Research Institute at Sheffield Hallam University has been represented in the Forum since 1997.

While Doug Liversidge began as Chairman of the Forum, the management structure was modified in 1995 with a co-chairman being elected from an industrial member company. By 1997, Liversidge was able to stand down, so that one academic and one industrialist were co-chairs. This established 'ownership' of the Forum amongst the member companies and university participants.

The remainder of this section looks in a little more detail at the structure and organisation of SMF before examining some examples of research collaboration and networking which it has initiated. The strengths and weaknesses of the Forum and what can be learned from it regarding university-industry interactions are outlined in the conclusion.

Structure and organisation

SMF's structure allows for interactions between the universities and member companies at a variety of different levels. There is an annual dinner and meeting of the Principal's group, which is chaired by the Vice Chancellor and is normally attended by the Managing Director or Technical Director of each company, along with senior staff involved in materials engineering and technology from the university side. This is seen as a very good opportunity for networking by the companies. Decisions about which projects to support through SMF funding are taken by a research co-ordination committee. This meets regularly and consists of senior technical managers from the firms, along with senior staff from the Sheffield engineering departments. When making decisions about project support, priority is given to those that can be shared openly amongst members of the Forum. Once a decision has been made to support a project, it is assigned a 'project champion', usually on the company side, whose job it is to ensure that the project delivers its objectives.

A number of these projects and other forms of interaction encouraged by SMF are described in more detail below.

SMEs and the local economy: building networks

While the emphasis of SMF is on large companies, detailed research was carried out on one SME for whom networking was an important reason for joining the Forum. The London and Scandinavian Metallurgical Co Ltd (LSM) is a supplier of intermediate materials, especially aluminium products to the metallurgical industry. It is a medium-sized company, with 400 employees and an annual turnover of £100 million.

In addition to the research agenda, one of the main attractions of the Forum for LSM is that all of the other member companies are their customers, providing an ideal opportunity for personal contacts to be developed, which could then be used to exchange information about LSM's products and how they could be improved. Managers from the company confirmed that, since SMF's inception, member companies were having contacts with each other outside of official Forum meetings to a much greater degree than they had done previously. In this respect, the Forum would seem to be achieving one of its initial objectives, which was to revive the tradition of close business contacts which once led Sheffield to be described as the 'biggest village in England'.

Despite benefiting from these opportunities, LSM managers thought that the Forum could perhaps do more to encourage SME involvement. The initial focus had been placed on large firms because, even in their case, there was little interaction prior to the Forum. The University of Sheffield's Regional Office does run a separate business network for SMEs in this sector called 'Materials Technopole' and also co-ordinates a highly regarded 'UNCLE' scheme, whereby SMEs are mentored by a large company in the same industry but with a different supply chain. However, more synergy could be created by establishing links of communication between these two structures, so that small companies have the opportunity to interact with their larger customers further up the supply chain in the way that a medium-sized company like LSM has done through the Materials Forum.

Product development and technology transfer

The research projects financed by SMF facilitate the transfer of technical expertise between the university and company sectors and sometimes enable the firms to develop more reliable and sophisticated products.

A case in point is a research project that involved collaboration between a PhD student in the Automatic and Control Systems Engineering Department at Sheffield and the British Steel Swinden Technology Centre. Based just outside Rotherham, the Swinden Technology Centre is one of British Steel's main centres of research and development. Its particular focus is on product development, both in terms of short-term responses to market needs and long-term strategic research into new techniques and technologies to ensure that the company's product base remains competitive.

The research project noted that specialist heat treatments are used to develop the required mechanical properties in a wide range of steels, titanium alloys and nickel-based alloys. Conventionally, this is achieved by hardening and tempering the material, which is in the form of rolled product or forgings. Adjustments in furnace temperatures help determine the final mechanical properties of a given steel analysis along with the necessary quench types. Variations in results can occur for a variety of reasons including prior thermo-mechanical treatment and variations in analysis.

Traditionally, the heat treatment metallurgist has been responsible for balancing these variables through the use of linear regression analysis. These techniques, however, impose restrictive assumptions on the form of relationships to be found in the data and non-linear methods, such as neural networks and fuzzy logic, are potentially more appropriate techniques in view of the data's complexity. The PhD student applied these technologies to the heat treatment process to predict the optimum thermal treatments and ultimately the mechanical properties. The final predictive model led to improved product quality and reduced process costs.

Another example of PhD research collaboration, which led to improved product quality and reduced process costs, concerned the analysis of cleanliness in steels. A major objective of steel manufacturers is to be able to characterise and quantify the cleanliness of steels. Some degree of impurity is inevitable, but if it contains large, concentrated quantities of impurities, this can adversely affect the integrity of the metal. Similarly, if there are small clusters of inclusions spread throughout the steel, this has negative consequences for properties such as ductility and fatigue. Techniques exist to find large inclusions in substantial quantities of steel and to quantify inclusion distributions in very small quantities, but this project was able to reduce the gap between the 'macroscopic' and 'microscopic' forms of testing. It analysed small samples by a variety of different techniques, compared the results and identified the most effective methods for prediction of the maximum inclusion size, consistent with acceptable levels of integrity, ductility and fatigue, in large volumes of steel. Predicting inclusion sizes in this way lessens the need to test large quantities of steel for impurities and thus makes possible both reductions in process costs and improvement in product quality. The project involved extensive collaboration with a number of SMF member companies, including British Steel Engineering Steels, British Steel Swinden Technology Centre, Avesta Sheffield and Special Melted Products.

IMMPETUS : combining applied research with academic excellence

The Department of Engineering Materials at Sheffield carries out research of the highest academic quality, receiving a 5* grade from the Metallurgy and Materials panel in the 1996 HEFCE Research Assessment Exercise, one of only eight departments to do so. A key part of the Department's research is conducted by the world-renowned thermomechanical processing research group. This subject area was of the most interest initially to the member companies of the Materials Forum, so that in 1993, a substantial fraction of the industrial funding was set aside to support the development of a Centre of Excellence, Formec, in this area. Over the next two years, the Centre spawned 17 collaborative research projects through the Forum and in 1995 formed the basis of a much larger collaboration, Immpetus, or Institute for Microstructural and Mechanical Process Engineering – a multi-disciplinary partnership bringing together the Departments of Automatic Control and Systems Engineering, Mechanical Engineering and Engineering Materials.

Immpetus carries out a small amount of applied research funded by research councils, government departments and industrial companies, but its primary objective is to provide the scientific underpinning for the development of physically based models to be used in the thermomechanical processing of metals. This combination of academic excellence with research areas that are industrially relevant provides a very powerful illustration of the strengths of SMF's approach but also, paradoxically, one of its main weaknesses.

The fact that the core researchers in this group, as with SMF as a whole, are heavily involved in fundamental research means that the scope for developing near-market collaborations with industry is limited. Certainly, nothing on the scale carried out by Warwick Manufacturing Group is attempted or achieved. While this is quite legitimate, as it allows the partnership to prioritise long-term, pre-competitive research, it does reduce the final impact of the partnership and SMF on the product and process development performance of its member companies and other organisations from the Sheffield area which might be tempted to join. As the example of WMG shows, companies become willing to invest large sums of money in research collaboration with universities when they are convinced that the university can help them to tangibly improve performance, especially in the areas of productivity and product development. This requires an emphasis, at least in the early stages, on contract research that delivers short-term benefits. While this is not a criticism of the quality of SMF's collaboration with industry, it does limit the scale and scope of interaction and therefore the Forum's ultimate impact on its client base.

Interim remarks – Sheffield

SMF is not an intermediate institution in the style of WMG. Industrial research and academic functions are not separated, which makes it hard to offer firms the guarantees about delivery and completion times that WMG can supply. This restricts the types of applied research they are able to carry out with firms and the scale of interactions they can sustain. SMF also suffers from the limitation that it has very few links with SMEs and needs to be linked more systematically to the Materials Technopole to provide a better service for this group. These limitations are outweighed, however, by the Forum's positive characteristics:

● Like WMG, SMF has benefited from being part of a university that has a very strong record of industrial links, especially in the tenure of the current vice-chancellor. This has provided a *university infrastructure* conducive to the development of collaboration with the business sector.

- SMF has *built up its industrial network* in a sensitive and responsive way, making sure that the members can make an input into the issues that are researched and, indeed, are closely involved in the projects. It has also made judicious use of an industrial champion to establish links with senior managers in the client base, which increases the chance that product development or process changes suggested by research projects will actually be implemented.

- It has built up an industrially relevant *research programme* by providing structures that enable member companies to make decisions about projects to support. Indeed, the companies are able to establish ownership over particular elements of the research programme, which helps to maintain their commitment to the process.

- SMF is *genuinely embedded in the regional economy*, having played an important role in re-creating a network in an important industrial district. The member companies now have contacts with each other that would not have occurred prior to SMF's formation and are starting to develop the kinds of co-operative links exhibited by industry-specific regional clusters in other parts of the world. This has potentially important long-term consequences for the economic performance of the group.

Conclusions – how does this inform policy?

This chapter has clearly demonstrated that there is a fruitful role for expanding university-industry links in more traditional, engineering based sectors and that these links can be usefully extended to include the regional economy and SMEs. The generic features of the model still hold true. As the examples of Sheffield and Warwick show, projects need to be managed commercially, informal and formal networks are important, as is a clear delineation of staff roles in research, teaching and consultancy. In addition, the role of a translator is key to making the effective transition from the university research base into product application.

However, the two case studies demonstrate that these features need some tailoring to the unique characteristics of manufacturing companies. In particular, neither university was conducting 'blue sky' research through spinouts that it then sought to commercialise. In the case of Warwick, applied research was defined by industrial clients and while this might have also had a 'blue sky' element, this was secondary to the desire for commercial returns (hence the relative paucity of published papers). In the case of Sheffield, the university sought to develop links with industry and deliberately embarked upon 'industry relevant' projects which are then disseminated through local networks.

What all this suggests is that, for manufacturing, the 'Partnership' type projects and building mutual understanding with the implicit goal of increasing company profitability, may be more appropriate. With this in mind, then, a number of common features need to be highlighted:

- *The importance of university-level support:* in both cases, support at a University level for greater links with industry was substantial and essential to making the partnership projects work. At Warwick, this support was evident through the University's tolerance of industry-standard pay scales and terms and conditions, while at Sheffield, support at the highest level has guaranteed the effective development of networks.

- *The importance of entrepreneurial academics:* both universities had dynamic individuals in charge of the industry-university links that provided the drive behind the projects.

- *The importance of client network management:* overcoming cultural resistance on the part of industry to the activities traditionally conducted by universities has been achieved at both institutions through education and training, professional project management and, critically, through the development of substantial networks of small and large companies from the local area. These networks serve the purpose of building trust, sharing experience and generating project ideas and incomes.

- *Staffing:* the Warwick example in particular illustrates the importance of providing adequate rewards and returns for staff taking a post within a university in the first place and, once there, pursuing industry-relevant activities. WMG pays industry competitive salaries and has clear career paths. This type of staff development potential provides incentives aside from the normal RAE accredited publications which means that their industry-based work is equally valued.

Policymakers, then, can learn in a number of ways from the research contained in this chapter. First, it is evident that more informal and flexible structures, based on networks and sharing of ideas are necessary in creating effective university-industry links in manufacturing-related sectors. This is not least the case since much of the research that is conducted is incrementally innovative rather than radical or 'blue sky' in nature and partnership projects are more suitable to the iterative nature of incremental innovation. Network structures are particularly important for SMEs in ensuring that trust is built within a 'safe' environment. Policies to encourage networks and development of mutual understanding, for example through the RDAs or through the research councils would be particularly effective here.

Second, the case of WMG pay structures underlines the importance of providing adequate recognition for industry-based work within universities. Individuals need to be encouraged into university research departments to play a role both as educators and as 'translators' in order to make results of research available to the widest possible audiences from large and small companies alike. Incentivising such activities must be a key area for policy.

Finally, and most importantly, both examples covered in this chapter demonstrate the importance of over-coming cultural barriers to partnerships. This has been operationalised differently in each institution, but the lessons for policy are clear: the real barrier to effective partnerships rests in mutual distrust. Policy must address this as a primary concern.

4. Construction and packaging

As with traditional engineering and manufacturing sectors, the scope for innovation within the construction and packaging sectors is likely to be incremental rather than radical in nature. In Chapter 3 it was suggested that incrementally innovative industrial structures are, perhaps, more suited to the 'partnership' type programmes since these have the specific function of improving customer performance through, for example, improved productivity or through product or process innovations. Using this framework, the discussion now turns to examples of university-industry links in the construction and packaging sectors with a view to providing extra weight to this statement.

Construction

Background to the sector

Despite technological developments of potential relevance to the industry, construction remains a labour-intensive sector. Within the UK especially, it is also one characterised by low levels of research and development spending. Whereas in Japan, construction companies spend about three per cent of sales revenue on R&D, in the UK it is 0.5 per cent (Gann, 1991). Also, whereas in Sweden there is extensive use of CADCAM technology in this sector, this remains a rarity in the UK. These factors are partly responsible for the UK's relatively low productivity in this sector.

A particular problem for the construction industry is its highly fragmented production process, with the different stages – commission, design, construction and maintenance – being hampered by poor communication between them (Gann, 1991). Whereas in some other countries, notably Japan and Sweden, these problems have been partially circumvented by a movement towards pre-fabrication, which reduces the number of stages in the process, the UK experiments with this in the 1960s and 1970s were associated with unpopular buildings of poor quality, so there is little prospect of a wholesale movement towards this reducing the communication problem. Considerable attention has been focused in the 1990s, however, on the potential for manufacturing production processes to be replicated in construction, so that the dramatic productivity growth enjoyed by some manufacturing sectors can be experienced. The notion here is that the integrated nature of production processes in manufacturing can in some way be applied in construction, to obviate the problem of fragmentation. Considerable weight is attached to this possibility by the Construction Task Force, which was convened by John Prescott to investigate ways of improving construction industry performance (Construction Task Force, 1998). The Innovative Manufacturing Initiative, funded jointly by the Engineering and Physical Sciences Research Council (EPSRC), Economic and Social Research Council (ESRC) and Biotechnology and Biological Sciences Research Council (BBSRC), has sponsored a number of projects under its Construction as a Manufacturing Process Programme.

One of the most innovative ways in which manufacturing processes can be transferred to the construction context is through the application of information technology. This is one of the aims of the Construct IT Centre of Excellence.

Construct IT Centre of Excellence

Construct IT is a national network of companies and university departments, interested in the application of information technology and management to the construction industry. Its primary goal is to co-ordinate and promote innovation and research in IT in construction in the UK, to improve the competitive performance of the UK construction industry. To this end, it brings together the leading contractors, clients, suppliers, consultants and computer/communication firms related to the industry with researchers from eight universities with expertise in the area. Set up in 1994, it is based at the University of Salford.

Inception and early stages of development

Construct IT came into being against the background of the construction industry's relatively poor economic performance, and the seeming reluctance of many large firms to recognise the extent of the problems. The key individuals responsible for the development of Construct IT were Peter Brandon, Pro-Vice-Chancellor for Research at the University of Salford and the late Geoff Topping, who in 1994 was the Chairman of Taylor Woodrow Construction, one of the UK's largest construction companies. They had worked together on a number of research projects prior to the formation of Construct IT and were strongly of the opinion that university-industry collaboration could play an important role in encouraging improved performance on the part of construction companies. In particular, Brandon was of the view that the construction industry had to harness the power of information technology if it was to overcome the fragmentation which characterised the industry – IT was thus the key factor for improving productivity in the industry (interview notes).

Each of the 'project champions' had sufficient credibility in their spheres of influence to convene a two-day meeting of many of the major UK construction companies and consultancies, along with the leading research universities in the built environment sector.

The construction companies were also motivated to attend by a fear of foreign competition and a lack of confidence in their ability to cope with it. The sector had, until the early 1990s, been spared the kind of intense international competition experienced by many areas of manufacturing, but had noted that, in countries such as Japan, manufacturing companies were penetrating the construction sector (Toyota was the fourth largest housebuilder in Japan in the early 1990s). The firms were keen, therefore, to understand the potential of IT as an integrating tool that might protect them from this threat. Topping was able to ensure that the firms were represented by their Chairmen or Chief Executives, a key factor for ensuring that the meeting was taken seriously by the company and a clear indicator that this was so. Brandon and Topping were also able to interest the Department of the Environment (DoE) in the meeting, since the DoE was attempting to encourage university-industry links itself when, in late 1994, it went ahead. It was as a result of this meeting that the decision was taken to create Construct IT. Professor Martin Betts of the Department of Surveying at Salford was appointed Director, a post he held until this year, when the job passed to Marjan Sarshar.

While Construct IT involves eight universities, it is based at Salford, which confers a number of advantages upon it as an institution aimed at linking firms with the knowledge base.

University background

The University of Salford has a long history of collaboration with industry.

> Established as a University from a College of Advanced
> Technology in 1969, and set at the very centre of the historic
> source of the world-wide industrial revolution in Manchester,
> Salford was bound to find an affinity with Britain's
> manufacturing base. At least that is the theory and there is more
> than a grain of truth in this statement. (Brandon, 1998:1).

As Brandon suggests, Salford's historical background pre-disposes it
towards industry, but it is events of the more recent past which have
cemented this relationship. Salford was faced with the need to make
financial savings at very short notice in the early 1980s. In 1981 it
faced a 43 per cent larger reduction in funding over three years than had
been expected (Ashworth, 1985). The response was to seek sources of
external funding, as well as to reduce costs. Decision-making was
expedited by the relatively compact nature of Salford's management
team, consisting of the vice-chancellor, Registrar and a small group of
Pro-Vice-Chancellors. By November 1982, the Senate had formally
approved a statement of aims and objectives for the university that
summarised and codified its conclusions under the three headings of
'Teaching', 'Research' and 'Technology and Skill Transfer' (Brandon,
1998). By the early 1980s, therefore, Salford had adjusted its mission
statement to take account of the 'third aspect – an economic
development role through outreach activities'. Furthermore,

> Not every member of staff could undertake the full portfolio of
> collaboration and it was recognised, by implication, that there
> needed to be parity of esteem between the three headings of
> teaching, research and technology and skill transfer. However,
> rewards should be there for demonstrable achievement in
> activities connected with the University's relations with industry
> as much as with conventional University activities. This in turn
> required recognition through the promotion procedures, career
> development schemes and the resource allocation models to
> ensure that the system supported vision. (Brandon, 1998:5).

Work with industry was incentivised within the university's reward structure. This, along with the other aspects of Salford's culture, make it a supportive environment in which to develop links with industry. This is clearly of benefit to Construct IT.

Structure and organisation

In addition to Salford, the university members of Construct IT are Loughborough, Nottingham, Reading, Sheffield, Strathclyde, UCL and UMIST. In each case, a construction-related department is involved and these represent all of the RAE 5-star rated departments in this field.

The industrial members are ABB Steward, Alfred-McAlpine, Allott & Lomax, AMEC, Advanced Visual Technology, BAA, Ballast Wiltshier, Balfour Beatty, Barclays Property Group, BDP, Bentley Systems, Binnie Black & Veatch , Birse Construction, BT Property, Boots, Bucknall Austin, CSB, Cadaim, Cap Gemini, Costain , Crest Nicholson, CSSP, Gallifords, Gleeds, HBG Kyle Stewart, IBM, Intergraph, John Laing, John Sisk, KPMG, Kvaerner, Leighton Holdings Construction, Masons, NG Bailey, Mercury, Norwest Holst, Sir Robert Macalpine, SAP UK Ltd, Siteman Software, Syntech, Tarmac, Taylor Woodrow, Tilbury Douglas, The Miller Group Ltd, Tweeds, Unisys, WS Atkins and Wates Construction. Each member company pays a subscription of £3,000 per annum. Whereas senior members of the Board were involved at the inception of Construct IT, the hands-on collaborative work tends to be carried out by the IT directors and managers of these companies. While the Department of the Environment, Transport and the Regions (DETR), as it is now called, supported the creation of Construct IT, it does not provide any core funding, but does recognise the institution for the receipt of research grants.

Collaborative work is carried out between the member universities and firms in accordance with the following remit:

- identify and commission research projects

- undertake and report on benchmarking studies

- promote postgraduate and continuing education

- define an IT research work plan

- compile a database of ongoing research as part of an industry knowledge base

- host international practice and theory conferences

- provide information about current industry best practice

- facilitate technology transfer

- ensure that a link exists between IT users and producers

- exploit shared visions in strategies and policy

- participate in pre-competitive research and development

- introduce practical and 'real world' influences into research

- strengthen existing influences in the industry

- obtain wider research funding

- explore leading-edge technology

Administratively, Construct IT is based in the Department of Surveying at Salford. It has a small Management Board, consisting of a Chairman and Deputy Chairman drawn from the industrial membership, along with representatives of construction industry clients, consultants, the IT industry and solicitors who specialise in construction sector. These representatives are also drawn, of course, from Construct IT member companies. The other Board members are the Director, Marjan Sarshar, and a Manager, who carries out a lot of the day-to-day running of the centre.

Two-day meetings of the membership are held biannually, at which reports and presentations are given on the collaborative research undertaken under the Construct IT banner. The research itself arises out of contacts between the industrial members and staff from the member universities, which either come about informally or are co-ordinated by members of the Management Board. The Board, especially the Chairman and Director, also take a proactive role in identifying potentially fruitful areas for collaboration. Where research projects go ahead, this will usually be with some financial support from the member companies involved, along perhaps with public funding from among the many programmes relevant to university-industry interactions (see Chapter 1).

One of the major themes of research initiated through Construct IT has been on construction as a manufacturing process. Some projects from within this area are described in detail below. The Centre has also been very effective at developing post-experience education courses similar to those characteristic of the Warwick Manufacturing Group. These are also examined.

Construction as a manufacturing process

Traditionally, the construction industry operates in a way where the different stages of a construction project are separate and work is performed consecutively. In addition, the industry has many disciplines and this makes the flow of information a critical factor in the efficiency of the industry. The participants in a construction project perform many tasks /activities during the life cycle of a project which involve the use of thousands of pieces of information. Such information is spread without any structure or classification across these disciplines. This leads to many problems in terms of information handling and management, as well as relating different pieces of information to each other. In a poor communication environment, changes at any stage may not be accounted for in another. For example, if the design is modified after the project planning stage, activities logic, durations and materials requirements tend to be greatly affected. As a result, the entire process is disturbed. In an integrated environment, such changes would be transferred directly as the information flow is consistent. The use of an integrated environment to integrate the information used by all parties would thus help rid the industry of the above problems and also bring other related benefits such as reducing lead times, reducing costs and improving quality (Kagioglou et al, 1998). This environment needs to be designed around a central integrated database (Aouad, 1994).

One project, initiated through Construct IT, which sought to facilitate such an integrated environment, was *Information/Integration for CONstruction (ICON)*. ICON was developed at the University of Salford in 1994 and was funded by the Science and Engineering Research Council (the predecessor of the EPSRC). It involved researchers from both IT and construction backgrounds and was assisted and guided by representatives from industry and professional institutes (Royal Institute of British Architects, Royal Institution of Chartered Surveyors, Chartered Institute of Building and National Building Specifications).

The ICON project introduced the subject of integrated databases to construction industry professionals. Such databases can be used as a means of integrating the various functions performed by these professionals. The study assessed the feasibility of the development of such databases from both IT and construction perspectives. It assessed the potential of existing techniques and used demonstrators to show the type of applications that can be integrated. The outcome of the study was a framework for an integrated database which could facilitate information sharing between the processes of design, procurement and management of construction (Aouad *et al*, 1996). This framework was enhanced by the OSCON project.

The *Open Systems for CONstruction (OSCON)* project was undertaken by the University of Salford, funded by the DoE, from 1995 to 1997. As with ICON, the project included the active involvement of a number of companies from various parts of the construction industry. OSCON built upon the results and conclusions of the ICON project by illustrating the benefits of the use of a centralised database for an integrated construction environment for a construction project. For this project only selected construction tasks were chosen for inclusion as it was only intended as a research prototype. Those included were architectural design, costs estimating and construction planning.

A suite of software was developed which actively shared construction project information from a central object-oriented database. This was achieved with the use of a central object-oriented information model that had two constituent parts. Namely, the domain models which support the integration from a specific domain, such as construction planning, and the core model which holds the knowledge of how information is transferred from one specific domain to other specific domain models. Both the domain and core models were abstracted to a higher level than specific software applications but the domain models were supportive for certain classes of application, such as project management or drafting software.

Both the ICON and OSCON projects used IT to develop software capable of integrating the construction process, using methods previously applied in manufacturing. By improving the quality of communication between the disparate parts of the construction industry, they make possible reduced lead times, lower costs and improved product quality. The most comprehensive attempt to consider construction as a manufacturing process, however, which has been generated through Construct IT, is the Process Protocol project.

The *Generic Design and Construction Process Protocol* project was funded by the EPSRC from 1996-98 under the Innovative Manufacturing Initiative. A wide spectrum of collaborating companies from the construction industry joined University of Salford researchers to carry out the project. These included clients, contractors, sub-contractors, architects and suppliers, many of whom provided funding for the research. As the title of the project suggests, its aim was to develop a Generic Design and Construction Process Protocol for the construction industry by considering the lessons learnt through a number of decades in manufacturing. The manufacturing examples had, of course, to be adapted to suit the specific conditions of construction and the project aimed to do this by comprehensive reviews of the construction and manufacturing industries, interactive workshops with the project industrial partners, case studies in the manufacturing and construction industry and other research and data collection tools and techniques.

The particular focus of the Process Protocol project was on the New Product Development (NPD) methods that have evolved in manufacturing in recent decades. Increased competition and product complexity, as well as dynamic customer requirements and legislative restrictions, have forced manufacturing companies to look for more effective and efficient ways for developing new products. Concurrent engineering (CE) has introduced the concept of overlapping activities, whereby two or more activities can be performed virtually simultaneously. Based on CE, a number of approaches have been developed, such as integrated product development and accelerated product development. They are all based on cross-functional integration and the concept of teamwork.

Of particular interest among these approaches is that of stage-gate systems (O'Connor, 1994). In this depiction, the product development process is presented as a series of gates and stages, which can vary from typically four to seven (Cooper, 1993) depending on the particular organisation that is using it. Each stage represents a number of activities that need to be performed and information that needs to be gathered to progress the project to the next gate. Stages do not represent single functional activities in the organisation but are multi-functional, involving a number of people from different departments relevant to the activities. Gates represent decision or Go/Kill points, which specify a set of criteria or 'deliverables' that the project must or should meet in order to proceed to the next stage of development. The gates serve as quality control checkpoints, and are usually controlled by senior managers from different functions, who own the resources that are required by the project leader or team. Stage-gate processes have been found to reduce development time, produce marketable products, and optimise internal resources by eliminating projects which are not promising (LaPlante and Alter, 1994; Anderson, 1993; Cooper and Kleinschmidt, 1991).

There are, though, a number of disadvantages and weaknesses associated with the stage-gate system. Cooper (1994) lists six deficiencies of the system:

- Projects must wait at each gate until all tasks have been completed. Thus, projects can be slowed down for the sake of one activity that remains to be completed.

- The overlapping of activities is not possible.

- Projects must go through all stages and gates, where in some circumstances it might be quicker to eliminate or bypass some activities, especially for small firms.

- The system does not lead to project prioritisation and focus, as it was originally designed for single projects (Griffin and Hauser, 1996).

- Some new product processes are very detailed, accounting for minute details of the process, and therefore making it hard to understand, manage and learn.

- Sometimes it tends to be bureaucratic, making the process too slow.

To overcome these deficiencies of the stage-gate system, Cooper (1994) suggested modifications to the approach developed within manufacturing. The main characteristic of her modified approach is the overlapping of the stages. Go/Kill decisions are delayed to allow for flexibility and speed, and the previously 'hard' gates are presented as 'fuzzy' gates, which can be either conditional or situational. Conditional gates relate to a 'Go' decision made subject to a task being completed at a specified point in time, and that the results of this task indicate that it is still a good project. Situational gates refer to a 'Go' decision being made when the information of the task that is not yet complete is not vital enough to halt the project. Due to the overlapping of stages, and for the sake of flexibility, decision-making authority will shift away from senior management and more towards the team and team leader. The use of 'fuzzy' gates is deemed more suitable to the less controlled production environment that exists in construction as compared to manufacturing, allowing as it does for more flexibility and devolved decision-making (Cooper, 1994).

The product development model produced by the Process Protocol project represents a considerable refinement of this approach and its systematic application to the construction industry. It breaks down the design and construction process into 10 distinct phases – demonstrating the need; conception of need; outline feasibility; substantive feasibility study and outline financial authority; outline conceptual design; full conceptual design; co-ordinated design, procurement and full financial authority; production information; construction; and operation and maintenance. These are separated by a combination of 'hard' and 'fuzzy' gates and can be enacted either sequentially or concurrently. A key role is envisaged for IT at each stage in the process (Kagioglou et al, 1998).

The Process Protocol project is widely regarded as having made considerable progress toward the establishment of a generic design and construction product development model, which applied the principles learned from manufacturing in a way which will encourage more integrated production processes in construction, with all the benefits this entails for reduced lead times, lower costs and improved product quality. This regard is reflected in the fact that the research team has won financial assistance from the EPSRC to carry out further development of the model.

Integrated Graduate Development Scheme (IGDS)

The University of Salford's Department of Surveying runs an Integrated Graduate Development Scheme (IGDS) in association with Construct IT. The IGDS was set up with funding from the

EPSRC. It was recognised that the construction industry needed an input of skills that would provide an efficient, competitive and profitable future. The Scheme draws on the knowledge of users and researchers in delivering its courses, with research and technology managers from Construct IT member companies often being heavily involved. Further development of technology has given the opportunity for delegates to study the courses fully distance learning via the internet as an alternative.

The IGDS is composed of the following courses:

- Industrial MSc, focusing on work related issues and problem solving projects with a final integrated project.

- Traditional MSc with a research bias and completion of a dissertation.

- Masters of Research (MRes) degree with advanced research methodology training and dissertation (intended as a preliminary to a PhD).

There is great flexibility in delivery. The course can be studied full/part time or via internet distance learning. All programme study materials are provided on CD with the option to study on-line via the course web site, (a format for printing the workbook is also provided). Students can take part in the online module discussions and the real-time debates on the web. Students can contact each other and read career histories on individual student web pages.

All work is submitted electronically and assessment grades are added to students' confidential folders directly by the tutors. There are service agreements to ensure quality in delivery; assessment; student contact and tutorials. Service to the student is consistent whether he or she attends or studies via the web.

The programmes options are as follows:

- Full time over one year with year-round access to a PC.

- Part time over three years with two-day seminars (per module) in Manchester, plus distance study and work based projects.

- Fully *distance learning* with interactive communication via the internet and work-based projects.

While the IGDS is still relatively new, there are some early signs that it is encouraging the kind of synergies between research and education that have characterised the post-experience education programmes developed by the Warwick Manufacturing Group.

Interim remarks

Construct IT is attempting to encourage university-industry research links in a sector characterised by low productivity, low research-intensity and a fragmented production process. As such, there is no realistic prospect of it developing, at least in the medium-term, anything like the degree and scope of interactions achieved by some institutions in the more technologically based industries we have examined. Nevertheless, it has made a promising start and its experiences could provide lessons for other university-based institutions looking to develop relationships with industry.

Packaging

Packaging is increasingly seen as an important strategic tool for brand differentiation, as well as a key means of achieving improved logistics efficiencies, yet, traditionally the industry has had low R&D investment and very little interaction with the public sector research base. While the industry remains relatively low-tech, there are growing pressures on the packaging supply chain to provide innovative technological solutions to current strategic issues:

- Tighter environmental and legislative demands.

- Consumer demand for more customised products, which require shorter runs of a wider variety of packaging types.

- Supply chain drives for reduced inventory and faster response times in order to increase efficiency and lower cost.

- Pressure to improve packaging functionality as a means of brand differentiation.

- The need to innovate as a means of achieving competitive advantage.

White Rose Faraday Partnership for Enhanced Packaging Technology

The White Rose Partnership was created following a successful bid for £1m from the EPSRC to fund research and technology aligned to the needs of the UK packaging industry. It is a partnership which brings together key companies from within the packaging supply chain; three research-based universities – Leeds, Sheffield and York; Pira International, a research and technology organisation which services the packaging industry; and Cambridge Consultants, a multi-client innovation company. It is one of four such Partnerships that were created in 1997. Given the extent of debate about the merits and demerits of the Faraday concept as a method of encouraging interaction between industry and public sector research, it is important to evaluate this pilot (Centre for the Exploitation of Science and Technology, 1995).

The aim of the White Rose Partnership (WRP) is to assist its member companies to meet these technological challenges through knowledge transfer from the science base.

Structure and organisation

The WRP involves researchers from each of the three universities, but is administered by the Research Support Unit of the University of Leeds. Participation in the Centre is on a membership basis, with a fee structure dependent on size of organisation. The standard annual fee is £5000, falling to £800 for firms with fewer than 250 employees. The member companies, most of which are large, are drawn from several areas of packaging and related activities, including polymer suppliers, inks and related materials, adhesives, board and laminate suppliers, converters, fillers and retailers. There are regular meetings of the university, Research and Technology Organisation (RTO) and company members, who are usually represented by their Research and Development (R&D) or technology managers.

Building the network

As was stated previously, the packaging industry has very little record of contact with universities and is not research-intensive. Indeed, there was very little evidence of collaboration between companies, beyond the normal trading links. Building up the corporate membership in this area, therefore, presented something of a challenge, but the process was assisted by two factors. First, the prospect of deciding how up to £1 million of research funding from the EPSRC, available over the first 18 months of the Partnership's existence, should be spent on the packaging industry, was a considerable pull-factor for many companies in the sector. Second, Pira has a considerable track record of working with companies in this sector and many of these joined the Partnership. This was one respect in which the structure of Faraday Partnerships, all of which involve at least one RTO, was important in developing business membership.

The Partnership organises regular workshops and meetings for the members, at which ideas for research collaboration can be discussed. Of more value, however, according to some interviewees, are the monthly dinners that are arranged. These provide a less formal environment and considerable networking opportunities for the corporate members. They were especially important in the early stages of the Partnership, when corporate members were 'feeling their way' in university links. There are now considerable signs of a stable group of partner companies being built up, with corporate membership up to 24 in 1999. Very few of these, however, are small and medium-sized enterprises (SMEs), despite the offer of a reduced subscription. This is of some concern given that Faraday Partnerships were designed specifically to facilitate technology transfer from the science base to SMEs, but perhaps not surprising given that even the large firms in this sector have a poor record of R&D and university interaction. It will probably be some time, therefore, before SMEs can be drawn in from the supply chain in any great numbers.

The research programme

The industrial members were consulted through workshops and meetings before the main elements of the Partnership's generic research programme were identified. According to the university staff, this was a rather protracted process because most firms had very little idea of the kinds of research issues they wanted explored. Again, this can be explained by a lack of research culture in the industry, which was manifest in the firms' lack of awareness of relevant technological developments.

Eventually, three priority research areas were identified:

- *Agile manufacturing* – providing the potential for rapid and customised response with reduced costs.

- *Enhanced functionality of material* – providing the basis for greater benefits in product and pack design.

- *Enhanced environmental sustainability of materials* – providing improvements in recyclability alongside weight and cost reductions.

The Partnership believed that collaborative research projects in these areas would be most likely to enable firms to meet the industrial challenges noted above. Part of the EPSRC funding of the Partnership (up to £150,000) was reserved for fully funding core projects whose results are made available to all members. These projects concentrated on the core research areas identified above and were pre-competitive in nature. The remainder of the £1 million was used in conjunction with support from industrial members to fund specific member projects. The results of these projects were only made available to those companies that have provided financial support for them and have been a mixture of pre-competitive and more near-market research. The role of PIRA and Cambridge Consultants has been important in sharpening the focus of the near-market work (interview notes). Some progress has also been made towards the longer-term objective of accessing further EPSRC funding and specific support schemes such as DTI LINK and support from the European Union. Over the first five years of the Partnership, it was anticipated that research would be commissioned on behalf of industrial members to the tune of £7.5 million. Two years into the Partnership, this goal remains realistic. The Partnership has also set up a Strategic Intelligence Network to define product and process development needs across the membership. This operates through networking meetings and workshops to identify key technologies. This Network is feeding in to the project development process, and identifying potentially fruitful areas for near-market collaborations.

The Partnership's research programme is not linked in any systematic way to the educational provision of any of the three universities. 'People transfer' is promoted through the use of Faraday Scholars, young technologists who gain work experience in both academic and industrial settings, but there is no large-scale education programme strongly linked to the research in the manner of Warwick Manufacturing Group or Construct IT. The powerful synergies demonstrated in these institutions suggest this is a weakness of the Partnership. According to WRP staff, the EPSRC showed little interest in these links when designing the Faraday blueprint.

Interim comments

Like Construct IT, the White Rose Faraday Partnership shows that it is possible for business-university research links to develop even in low-tech sectors. With the Partnership only two years old, however, it is not possible to reach anything more than tentative conclusions about the effectiveness with which it has done this, nor to make definitive assessments of the Faraday concept on the basis of these conclusions.

Conclusions for policy

Once again, the material from this chapter has clearly demonstrated the case for enhancing university-industry links. First, where centres are based in universities there is an obvious need from the material in this, and other, chapters for a supportive environment at the highest level. This refers both to the need for 'support in principle' and, critically for more pragmatic support in the form of adequate incentive structures to encourage staff in an academic environment.

Second, both the Construct IT and WRP projects re-inforce the point that networks are important in the development of trust and understanding between partners and in developing appropriate research projects. In this context, the decision by the DTI to include a strong networking component into the evaluation of proposals under the second round of Faraday Partnership bids is greatly welcome. However, it is important that these networks are not simply with R&D personnel. The White Rose Partnership had contacts predominantly with R&D managers rather than with Managing Directors of local businesses. The effect was to restrict commercial opportunities offered by partnership research.

Third, the importance of education and training in breaking down cultural barriers should not be under-played. The role of teaching is central to Construct IT and extra projects and networks have developed as a result. Indeed, a major weakness of the White Rose Partnership was that it did not (at the time of the research) have obvious links into the teaching function of its partner universities which acted as a brake on informal networking activities. Policy must take into account the need for explicit links into the teaching function in order to enhance industry-university links.

5. Communications

The university-industry collaborations analysed above have mostly involved firms in manufacturing. It is well known, however, that the relative importance of this sector has declined markedly since at least the 1970s, both in terms of output and employment shares. In contrast, the service sector has come to account for an increasingly large proportion of output and employment

The services sector is of course very diverse and we concentrate here on the growing communications sector. This sector has some unique characteristics which affect the nature of any collaborative relationships between university and industry:

- It has enormous potential as a contributor to GDP not only in equipment manufacture and service delivery but also in enhancing efficiency and productivity in other industries. The UK is amongst the world leaders in mobile and personal communications, with particular strengths in mobile networking and service provision.

- In addition, the UK has succeeded in attracting significant inward investment and making strategic alliances in the areas of network infrastructure and terminal manufacture.

- This reflects the global nature of this sector as it is currently developing. Its companies are often very large and very powerful and operate internationally rather than nationally.

- The sector is highly research intensive both in industrial and academic institutions. However, particularly in the university community, this resource is scattered around a large number of small groups working in isolation. As a result, companies are often unaware of the existence of potentially valuable research effort and thus do not exploit it. Moreover, a number of university departments have specialised in communications research orientated towards the personal communications speciality. These have built up substantial research teams who enjoy support from the Engineering and Physical Sciences Research Council (EPSRC) and companies but continue their research programmes separately and in an unco-ordinated way.

However, they have the potential to work together and with industry within the framework of a single research project from which the output would exceed that achievable by the groups working separately.

These features of university research in mobile and personal communications were noted by the Technology Foresight Communications panel, which recommended that the research resources of the principal university departments should be co-ordinated to combine their efforts in a centre of excellence. This became the Virtual Centre of Excellence in Mobile and Personal Communications.

Virtual Centre of Excellence in Mobile and Personal Communications (Mobile VCE)

Set up in 1997, Mobile VCE is the operating name of the Virtual Centre of Excellence in Mobile and Personal Communications. It is a collaborative partnership between more than twenty of the world's most prominent mobile communications companies and seven UK universities each having long standing specialist expertise in relevant areas.

Research programme

Mobile VCE is a collaborative partnership engaged primarily in advanced, long-term pre-competitive research in mobile and personal communications. This is carried out in a variety of ways. Its main activities are embraced in its core research. This is a programme of advanced research undertaken in a distributed manner throughout all seven-member universities, under the guidance of nominated experts drawn from the industrial members. The core research is divided into four work areas:

- Networks
- Services
- Terminals
- Radio environment

The core programme commenced formally in April 1997 and will extend over a three-year period. Approximately 60 per cent of the work is funded by Mobile VCE from its members' subscriptions, while the remaining 40 per cent has been provided by the Office of Science and Technology (OST).

The total cost of the core programme is in excess of £3 million and is closely guided by the industrial members to ensure its continued relevance. This is carried out by four steering groups, one for each work area, consisting of small groups of identified experts chosen from among the member companies, who undertake this task on behalf of Mobile VCE as a whole. The work area steering groups are each chaired by a senior industrial representative and meet between four and six times a year. The research team is directly co-ordinated by an academic co-ordinator for each work area, who is also a full member of the relevant steering group. On a less frequent basis, meetings are convened of the academic co-ordinators and industrial chairmen of all four work areas with the Mobile VCE management to ensure consistency across the whole of the Programme.

The results of the Programme are disseminated to members in a variety of ways. One of the main ways is through the members only section of Mobile VCE's website, which provides news of progress milestones and successes, offers synopses of current reports and key deliverables, and provides a means by which members may request full copies of such reports in a variety of formats. In addition to the written medium, members' seminars occur on a twice-yearly basis to allow a fuller interactive involvement of members' personnel with the project teams.

In addition to the core programme, Mobile VCE commissions and manages contract research on behalf of one or more industrial members. This is usually carried out by a team of academic members, and is typically of shorter-term relevance than the core research. It offers members the advantage that the same collaborative agreements as are used for the core research may also be employed for contract research, which affords a significant saving in time and expense in initiating such work. It is planned in the future to offer a broadening range of services to industrial members, including the co-ordination of specialist professional training, technical consultancy and other advisory services.

Structure and organisation

Unlike the other university-industry collaborations we have analysed, Mobile VCE is a limited company. All Members are guarantors to the business, each with limited liability. The governing body is the General Meeting, which takes place at least annually but usually three times per year. Industrial members pay an annual subscription consisting of one or more 'units', each unit conferring a single vote at the General Meeting. The rate of subscription is £25,000 per unit and the maximum allowable units are four. There are 23 industrial member companies, which includes virtually every major mobile and personal communications company operating in the UK. A new category of associate industrial member has recently been created, which has reduced rates of subscription aimed at companies with less than 250 employees. There are seven academic members – the universities of Bradford, Bristol, Edinburgh, King's College London, Southampton, Strathclyde and Surrey. Academic members do not pay subscriptions but are entitled to vote at General Meetings. Industrial and academic members have the same status. The Department of Trade and Industry (DTI) and EPSRC are ex-officio members of the Board but do not have voting rights.

An Executive Committee is delegated by the General Meeting to undertake statutory control of the business, members of the Executive serve as legally responsible Directors of the company. Academic Members nominate three Directors to the Executive Committee, while another five Directors represent Industrial Members. One of the Directors is appointed to serve as Chairman. A full-time Executive Director, who is also the designated Chief Executive, performs day to day management of the company.

Conclusions

Mobile VCE has only been in existence for two years but it is possible to draw the following conclusions from its experiences:

- Its status as a limited company, with the associated allocation of legal responsibilities, ensures that the Centre is managed in a professional way, which is partly why it is able to attract high quality, innovative businesses to its industrial membership. It may be that, once university-industry collaboration involves the levels of industrial funding received by Mobile VCE, management structures more reminiscent of the private sector are appropriate.

- The main reason why Mobile VCE is able to charge £25-100k for corporate membership is because a high level of demand exists in the mobile and personal communications industry for research which may promote technological innovation. The industry's products have a high technological component and being able to understand and carry out technological innovation is essential to firms' ability to compete in the sector. While it is difficult to replicate these levels of demand across the board, this does show the importance of encouraging firms to appreciate the need for innovation and to compete on product quality.

- The idea of creating a virtual centre, whereby the expertise of leading universities in the sector is pooled and the Centre does not have a physical base, is one of potentially wide applicability. It is comparatively rare in any industrial sector for there to be one, or even two universities, which have sufficient expertise to be able to sustain a substantial amount of collaboration with industry. Pulling in experts from a range of universities creates a critical mass and range of intellectual ability that is able to carry out a detailed and varied programme of research. Avoiding a physical base for the Centre also reduces the extent to which the collaboration becomes associated with one particular university, which can lead the other universities to become less involved than they would otherwise. This problem has affected Construct IT and, to a lesser extent, Sheffield Materials Forum, amongst interactions we have analysed.

- On a less positive note, the model of intermediate institution represented by Mobile VCE does not have all of the features we have identified as being strongly associated with successful knowledge transfer. The staff of academic members who participate in the Centre continue with their other university duties, which restricts the type of interaction in which they can become involved. There is no explicit attempt made to link education and research. Attempts are being made to increase SME involvement, but so far these have not proved very successful.

6. International comparisons

With British policy arguably still seeking direction in the area of technology transfer, the extent to which alternative models can be imported into a British context needs to be assessed. It is the purpose of this chapter to review the German and American systems and to discuss their transferability. Both systems have been admired, albeit for different reasons, and British policy has taken lessons at various times from both structures. This in itself represents a justification for some form of international benchmarking against our major competitors.

One proviso is worth mentioning here, however. By definition, national structures evolve over time and in accordance with the needs of indigenous industry. Thus Germany, for example, has quasi-co-ordinated structures defined by the social market economy which developed after the second world war while the US 'system' is market based in essence. This means that any lessons that can be learned have to be generic in nature. The model developed in the introductory chapter provides a means of understanding university-industry links and technology transfer in the UK. Any policy recommendations must be made to fit within this structure.

Germany

A full discussion of the system of innovation in Germany falls beyond the scope of this report and of the research generally. Suffice it to say that the R&D and technology transfer systems reflect the complexity of the tripartite structures of the social market economy:

> In Germany science and technology planning, policy-making and funding take place on such a wide variety of different levels, and there are so many institutional structures, that it is difficult to avoid over-simplification when one tries to draw a coherent map of the present system... Not only do we have a wide variety of institutional actors, but within each institution we also find quite diversified structures funded by a multiplicity of sources and consisting of many sub-systems (Krull and Meyer-Kramer 1996).

This section looks at the R&D and technology transfer systems: the macro-level policies designed to stimulate research and development and the micro-level technology transfer between the science base and its commercial use through an intermediary. Of particular interest for the purpose of this report is the role of the Fraunhofer Gesellschaft (FhG), whose importance, particularly in mechanical and civil engineering and electronics is hard to overstate. However, in the 'new' technological areas of biotechnology, it may be that new structures are emerging. This is raised at the end of the section as a focus for further research.

Funding of the German research and technology systems – an overview

In 1996, Germany invested some 2.3 per cent of GDP in R&D activity, or DM 80.4 billion (BMBF 1998). This compares to a figure of 2.5 per cent of GDP in the US and is a net decline on the relative figure for 1989 of 0.6 per cent of GDP. A breakdown of this expenditure is shown in Tables 6.1 and 6.2. Table 6.1 gives data for R&D expenditure by source of funding. Thus, for example, government funding includes expenditure at regional and national level for all publicly funded projects, including for higher education and intermediate technology transfer institutes. Table 6.2 breaks R&D expenditure down by origin of research. Thus higher education establishments are a separate classification.

Table 6.1 German R&D expenditure (1992-1996)

	1992	1993	1994	1995	1996
Total R&D expenditure (BDM)	76.4	76.7	77.2	79.4	80.7
R&D spend as % GDP	2.48	2.43	2.33	2.28	2.26
of which					
Government*	36.0%	36.6%	37.1%	37.4%	37.3%
Non-profit Private sector	0.4%	0.3%	0.4%	0.4%	0.4%
Foreign origin	1.6%	1.7%	1.7%	1.8%	1.7%
Industry	62.0%	61.4%	60.9%	60.5%	60.6%

* This figure includes state (Länder) and federal government funding as well as funding from German Research Association and other quasi-public organisations. Länder fund roughly 46 per cent of total government support for R&D while the Federal Government accounts for 54 per cent (Krull and Meyer-Kramer, 1997).

Source: BMBF 1998

The 'dual' delineation of funding between industry and government is clearly illustrated by comparing the tables. Table 6.1 shows that roughly 60 per cent of funding for R&D comes from private sector industrial sources. However, industrial R&D accounts for considerably more than 60 per cent when calculated by the origin of R&D activity (ie where R&D is actually performed) as shown in Table 6.2.

Table 6.2 Sources of German R&D expenditure (1992-1996) by %					
	1992	*1993*	*1994*	*1995*	*1996*
Government & non-profit private*	14.3	15.1	15.0	15.5	15.4
Higher education	17.3	18.0	18.7	18.9	19.0
Industry	68.5	66.8	66.3	65.6	65.8

* Includes Helmholtz Centres, Max Planck Society, Fraunhofer Society, Blue List Institutes, State Institutes and other publicly chartered institutions (see Figure 6.1).

Source: BMBF 1998

The general system: an overview

There is a 'linear cascade' structure that exists in the German technology transfer system (Hohn und Schimanck 1991, Hohn 1998). The structure originated to ensure three things: independent basic scientific research (through the Max Planck Institutes), large scale structures for 'Big Science' of national or strategic importance and transferability through intermediate applied research institutes to the end industrial users. This is illustrated in Figure 6.1 below.

Basic research is conducted largely by the institutes of the Max Planck Society and by higher education institutions (HEIs). Core funding at this basic level is largely from the Länder (either individually or from the 1964 agreement). 'Paradigmatic' or strategic research is conducted by large laboratories, government research institutes and 'Blue List' task-oriented and large-scale research institutes funded on a 50-50 basis by the Federal Government (Bund) and the Länder. Applied ('post paradigmatic') research is conducted by technology transfer institutes, most notably the Fraunhofer, and funded jointly by Bund, Land and Industrial sources on a contract basis.

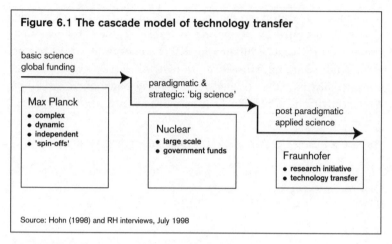

Figure 6.1 The cascade model of technology transfer

basic science
global funding

paradigmatic &
strategic: 'big science'

Max Planck
- complex
- dynamic
- independent
- 'spin-offs'

post paradigmatic
applied science

Nuclear
- large scale
- government funds

Fraunhofer
- research initiative
- technology transfer

Source: Hohn (1998) and RH interviews, July 1998

The R&D System: further details of funding and structure

Figure 6.1 hides the complexity of government funding for technology transfer, however. The actual organisation of the German R&D system is illustrated in Figure 6.2 below.

To argue that the system is complex is something of an understatement as is clearly illustrated by Figure 6.2. Above this structure are the Länder and the Federal Government, the National Science Council and the Conference of Ministers for Cultural Affairs, Education, Arts and Science. These supervisory bodies set funding targets and priorities.

Despite the complexity of the technology transfer and funding structure, however, funding priorities are clearly defined according to the targets set at a Federal level. These priorities are set irrespective of the nature or source of funding. Some targets are not set according to priorities but are focused on particular R&D performers (for example the FhG) who have autonomy in the allocation of funds to priority areas identified by demand (BMBF 1996, Teil III).

German R&D remains concentrated in traditional manufacturing industries: automobiles, electrical and non-electrical machinery, electronic and communication equipment and industrial chemicals (Abramson et al 1997). The result is patenting activity that is clearly focused in these areas of traditional economic strength (Cantwell and Harding 1998). For constitutional reasons, there has been very little R&D in defence related areas and aerospace (just eight per cent and six

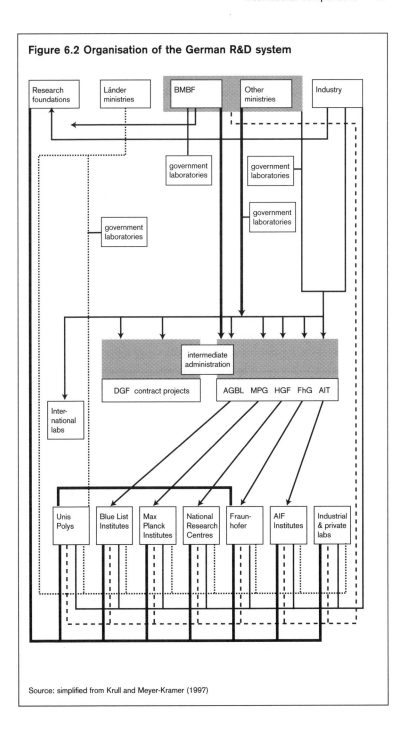

Figure 6.2 Organisation of the German R&D system

Source: simplified from Krull and Meyer-Kramer (1997)

per cent of the total budget respectively). As has been referred to above. German companies were, until recently, not permitted to undertake biotechnology research in general and genetic research in particular for similar reasons. This is reflected in the large number of firms which own overseas companies who conduct this research for them (this is particularly noticeable in the German ownership of small US biotechnology companies) (Cantwell and Harding 1998).

Evaluation of the system

Critics of the German system argue that it is top-heavy, complex and unresponsive. The cascade system illustrated in Figure 6.1 might appear organised and highly successful in some areas (for example, nuclear technology and environmental research), but it has noticeably failed to succeed in leading edge technologies like IT (Hohn 1998, Mason and Wagner 1998). The cascade structure was developed to separate out the private and public sector beneficiaries of scientific research. In areas like nuclear and environmental research the distinction between 'public goods' and private profit is relatively easily made and this is reflected in the sources of funding for such research within Germany. In IT, where technological change is rapid and private returns to innovation very high, the beneficiaries of research are less clearly delineated. Thus a technology transfer system based on an assumption that there is a clear delineation between the two which can be reflected in funding is bound to be relatively weak in radical innovation.

Criticisms such as this have resulted in changes to the funding structure, which are now beginning to emerge. Universities are gaining increasing proportions of their research funding from industry (rising from four per cent to eight per cent of total funding for basic scientific research and up to 20 per cent of the total funding for applied research). They are increasingly competitive with, for example, the FhG for industry funded contract research. A FhG scientist costs approximately DM 22,000 per month per project (including insurance, travel and subsistence, overheads and salary costs). Indeed, some estimates of FhG costs are as high as DM 35,000 per month. In contrast, a university scientist will cost around DM 12 000 per month as the university pays overheads. The qualifications of the two scientists are the same and so increasingly companies contract research from the universities. The AN-institutes (contract research establishments affiliated to universities and Fachhochschulen and with a particular focus on biotechnology and IT research) are a product of this new competitive environment (Technologie Nachrichten, März 1998).

It would be unwise to discount the cascade system as irrelevant in a world characterised by radical innovations, however. Incremental product innovation will always be important as radical scientific research develops into marketable products. The German economy has historically proved itself resilient to major shifts in techno-economic paradigms and there is no reason to suggest that the latest phases of IT or biotechnology should be any different:

- Institutions have existed within the German technology transfer system that reflect the market-based incentive structures that support radical innovation. For example, AN-Institutes (university-affiliated applied research centres) are emerging in the late nineties as major sources of dynamism and comparative advantage in innovation. These structures are not new, however. AN-Institutes were first established in the mid-1970s to plug the perceived hole in the cascade model that meant that prototypes were not reaching the market as viable products. The AN-Institutes, funded largely by contract research, were given clear incentives to assist in the production of such marketable goods. The contract research funding of AN-Institutes, and even of Fraunhofer, is still not risk capital in that the research institutes are non-profit organisations. However, this does not preclude the dynamic of profit-type incentives since many of the AN-Institutes have subsidiary limited liability companies affiliated to them.

- Large companies further exhibit this 'externalisation of risk' at a corporate level by technological 'outsourcing'. The example of biotechnology has been given above. Partnerships with small venture capital companies, frequently but not exclusively based abroad, allow large companies to concentrate on core businesses but simultaneously to develop new technologies. The domestic biotechnology market is, accordingly strengthening (Casper, 1998).

- While large companies conduct, say, biotechnology research through small venture capital companies, technology transfer institutes, like Fraunhofer and AÑ-Institutes, conduct research and develop prototypes in equipment manufacture which will allow them to compete even in the newly emerging technological markets. Thus, for example, medical instrumentation and diagnostic equipment are expanding areas of research in Max Planck, Fraunhofer and AN-Institutes.

- A system of pre-competitive research 'sharing' exists through the Industrial Research Associations (AiF). These are groups of SMEs who, unable to fund applied research themselves, join together jointly to participate in pre-competitive research leading to prototype development. Although much of this collaborative research is arguably *competitive* (Schmoch 1996), the AiF are an increasingly important structure within the system since they provide networks which span the technology transfer system, and provide access to innovation and hi-tech markets which would otherwise be out of reach for many small companies. The AiF structure is argued to counter-balance the *de facto* large company focus of Fraunhofer and Max Planck Institutes.

- Further 'networking' systems at a regional level exist through the Steinbeis Foundations, first established in 1971. These are applied research and consultancy units, which exist within HEIs, particularly Fachhochschulen. The major concentration of individual Steinbeis Technology Transfer Centres is within Baden-Würrtenburg but the Steinbeis Foundation's networks extend across Germany and abroad, especially in Europe. Their role in effective technology transfer is heavily debated. A technology transfer centre is usually led by a Fachhochschule Professor and staffed largely by students (usually writing final year or post-graduate dissertations). The projects are small and the companies using the Steinbeis service are usually from a 20-30km radius of the Centre. But, despite the controversial nature of the Steinbeis, they undeniably fulfil an important role in networking and knowledge sharing.

- Policy is changing to encourage overseas and domestic R&D back into Germany, while increasing emphasis is being placed on the area of biotechnology research. The whole funding structure of the German R&D system in general and technology transfer in particular is becoming more competitive with traditional 'quasi-monopolies' of public funds, such as the FhG, increasingly competing with a range of higher education and dedicated research institutes for funding.

● Finally, any suggestion that the thrust of Fraunhofer work is supportive rather than developmental, hides the capacity of the Fraunhofer to re-invent itself. Each Fraunhofer institute has a different character and a unique 'tacit knowledge' pool. Faced with the competitive threat of the equally qualified but cheaper AN-Institutes, co-operative structures have developed between and within Fraunhofer Institutes which are evolving to avoid duplication and, hence, to reduce overheads but which also integrate the combined strengths of the whole system.

Changing customer specifications and the perceived importance of radical innovation render the system prone to criticism, but it does appear to have a capacity to anticipate change. Thus, the system is proving remarkably resilient to major structural change while adapting incrementally to the external forces that require it to change. The Fraunhofer, for example, has structural advantages in its size and its focus on technology foresight. Funding in Germany is still for 'scientific excellence' and remains substantial. The 'emergent', although not new, technology transfer structures serve the interests of Mittelstand companies perhaps better through their networks, co-operation and competition with one another. These are also the structures that favour radical innovation. And in no sector of the technology transfer system is there evidence of shortage of funds – indeed, since Fraunhofer and AN-Institutes are non-profit making organisations, some representatives complained of having 'too much money'!

The role of the Fraunhofer Society

Funding and Structure

Within the context of the whole R&D system illustrated in Figure 6.1 above, the Fraunhofer may seem a relatively small part. But with 8,900 employees (of which almost one half are scientists and engineers), a total budget of DM 1.3 billion in 1996 and nearly 50 years in applied R&D and technology transfer, the organisation can not be described as insignificant. During 1995-6 it grew by 200 employees, increased its total contract research by nine per cent and increased total non-government funding by 16 per cent. The overall increase in core funding allocated to research was three per cent, a figure which compensates for the heavy loss of public project funding which fell to less than 16 per cent during 1995-6.

The Fraunhofer Gesellschaft zur Förderung der angewandeten Forschung (FhG) is a network of some 48 separate institutes of which there are some 36 in the old States of Germany and 12 in the new, east German states. Further, the FhG is establishing itself as a major intermediate technology transfer institution abroad. For example, in the United States, Brazil and China the FhG presence is particularly strong and supportive of both indigenous industry and of German companies operating overseas.

FhG institutes are established on the basis of perceived demand for contracted project research. An institute can be established if it can demonstrate that it will be able to achieve the required two-thirds of contract funding through project work over the next three years. Thus, for example there are just seven institutes that focus on microelectronics research in Germany because demand is small while demand in mechanical engineering is relatively high in Germany (reflecting the technological strengths of its indigenous industry) and, hence accounts for a larger number of institutes. Environmental technologies are strong in the FhG portfolio but biotechnology is relatively weak. Of its 48 institutes, all bar six have civilian R&D as their focus.

The Fraunhofer are particularly, although not exclusively, strong in supporting the needs of Small and Medium Sized Enterprises (SMEs). They act as catalysts for technology transfer between basic science and industry by providing scientists who work on the development of product prototypes based on new innovations in laboratories and higher education establishments. This is effected through the close contacts that FhG scientists have with research scientists in universities.

It is further aided by the contacts that the FhG have beyond the immediate technology transfer system into the wider innovation and corporate governance systems referred to above. For example, the Deutsche Bank has long acknowledged the structural weakness of the German financial system in encouraging venture capital projects, particularly from SMEs. Thus, it now pays the FhG a consultancy fee (estimated at around DM 20,000 per project) for its scientists to evaluate venture capital-type proposals (Kluth and Andersen 1997).

The role of Fraunhofer Institutes

Expectations of the FhG are high: that its institutes will, 'contribute to the innovative strength of the German economy' through the

- identification of innovative potential by keeping abreast of technological developments.

- meeting demands of industry for long term contract research and technical assistance.

- adapting tools and competencies to meet general research needs, including conducting research for public sector clients. (Krull and Meyer-Kramer 1996)

Thus a FhG scientist has a unique role as both a researcher and a scientific consultant. In principal, the scientist will not advise per se but will work on applied research with a practitioner (say from the end user) with the objective of balancing practical need with scientific feasibility. Consultants are employed separately to establish market need and design and develop products beyond a prototype stage.

This facilitating role, combined with the scientific and practical expertise of FhG researchers means that, despite increased competition, the FhG has comparative advantage in effective technology transfer between basic science and research which is further enhanced by its Foresight programmes and its patenting evaluation activities. Thus, although the subject expertise of a university and a FhG scientist may be identical, the latter has cumulative competence in the technology transfer relationship between the science base and the end practitioner. This cumulative expertise is strongest in the traditional areas of focus within the German economy and the role of the FhG scientists is arguably to re-inforce traditional areas of strength rather than to develop new ones.

Increasingly, however, universities, and particularly the Technische Fachhochschulen are gaining strength (and funding) both in the traditional areas of technology transfer and in new areas such as biotechnology. The relationship between consultants and scientists on a technology transfer project is not always clearly delineated and companies are beginning to require product development as part of the research contract.

The FhG is losing its monopoly of government funding, but argued one interviewee, 'you can't just get rid of 50 years of expertise'. With a dynamism that would answer the sternest critic, the FhG is changing to incorporate the dynamism of markets and the cumulative expertise of collaboration. Its newest institutes, such as the Technologie-entwicklungsgruppe (TEG) in Stuttgart do focus on product development and are more market-based in their outlook. It does have an increasing presence in biotechnology research and, like its corporate counterparts, is increasingly internationalising its activities in order both to support German companies abroad and to provide a model of technology-transfer to overseas companies in their own environment.

As the complex structure of Figure 6.2 shows, there is more to the German technology transfer system than simply the Fraunhofer Society. Interest in the literature as well as in policy circles has tended to focus on the strengths and weaknesses of the Fraunhofer for three reasons:

- because it is a unique intermediate technology transfer/bridging institution,

- because it is the largest such structure in Germany, and

- because historically it has had close links with both the science base in universities and other HEIs, with industrial applications and, critically, with the public sector.

However important the Fraunhofer may still be, it has increasingly been competing for public and private sector money with other structures within the technology transfer system. These institutes and structures are equally as well, sometimes better, connected with the science base and are frequently cheaper since their overheads are lower. The most relevant of these institutes from the viewpoint of British policy interest are the AN-Institutes.

AN-Institutes

AN-Institutes (research and technology institutes attached to universities) are, perhaps, the most readily transferable structures from the German technology transfer system into a British policy context since they are similar to the more market-based university-industry Research Centres that exist in the United States. They receive just ten per cent core funding (largely to cover accommodation) with the rest being provided by public and private contract research. Although they are non-profit making organisations, they frequently run spinout, hi-tech companies that are free to exploit any innovations and patents commercially. They take leading academics in relevant areas on two to five year secondments and provide research in leading edge technologies, in technology transfer (product and process technologies) and in organisational best practice.

The strengths of an AN-Institute depend on the strengths of the university or HEI to which it is attached:

- The Rheinisch-Westfalische technische Hochschule Aachen (RWTH) is, according to one interviewee within another organisation, putting forward a model of best practice for this type of structure. Its 'Forum-Informatik' uses some 60 professors from all disciplinary backgrounds in RWTH to produce leading edge technologies in IT working with partners from the public and private sectors. But it also is developing strength in biotechnology and biosciences (particularly biochemistry) using similar techniques.

- The AN Institute at the University of Freiburg is a leading world centre in solar technologies, despite reputed organisational difficulties. It accounts for 90 per cent of all patents in this research area, although all applications and sales of the technology are in the US.

- Biotechnology is strongly represented in AN-institutes at the Universities of Mannheim and Munich.

- Stuttgart University has strengths in engineering and manufacturing because of its links with industry in the region. Hence, the AN-Institute there (ISW), which was established in 1965 does basic and applied research in control technologies, machine tools and manufacturing systems. It is, according to one Fraunhofer interviewee, the major competitor to IPA since it is cheaper and technologically more advanced. It is much larger than FZI (see below): its organisational structure spans four departments and 13 separate research groups. But, like FZI, it draws heavily on students for applied and basic research projects. The composition of its turnover is similarly typical of the AN-institutes and is illustrated in Table 6.3 below.

Table 6.3 Activities of ISW-Stuttgart	
Area	% of turnover
Industrial projects	22
Public-private sector collaboration	29
Teaching/university activities	7
Basic research and public funding	42

All institutes advertise the public and private sector collaborative nature of their research and all emphasis that their research is 'leading edge' in nature.

Although AN-institutes have been visible in the German system for some 30 years now, it is only in the last five to ten years that their true potential has begun to be realised. They were established with a far broader remit than most Fraunhofer Institutes and are, hence, not limited to prototype development. Their research therefore tends to be far more commercially oriented with an emphasis on industrial application and exploitation. As a result, they tend to be far more radical in their research, take greater risks and have a far greater focus on 'fast-growing' technological areas like IT and biotechnology. Since government policy increasingly favours radical innovation, their strength and dominance is likely to increase.

A brief evaluation and comparison with Fraunhofer

The AN-institutes seem driven by customer technological requirements, which they interface with the expertise of the HEI to which they are attached. Unlike the Fraunhofer Institutes, their overheads are low and their dependence on the traditional and more bureaucratic structures of the German innovation system almost non-existent. Indeed, their dependence on this system comprises of two things: the ten per cent (or less) funding from a regional government which gives them accommodation and the requirement that they do not make profits from their technology transfer activities.

In effect this means that their focus has to be on transferring technology to SMEs since any residual money from contract research can be used to cross-subsidise workshops or seminars. And, since the researchers within the AN-institutes are able to exploit their own research by creating spin-off companies from product or process innovations, the AN-Institute structures have the potential to produce radical innovations in the way the UIRCs do in the US.

And yet there is no reason to suggest that the AN-Institutes will overtake the Fraunhofer as the leading technology transfer structures within the German innovation system. This is the case for several reasons:

- The AN-Institutes are regionally based despite their more 'global' focus on fast-growing technologies since they are attached to a university or HEI. There is substantial collaboration between AN-institutes in different regions, but there is no national umbrella structure, which would provide regulation and homogeneity as with the Fraunhofer. In consequence, the focus on hi-tech will remain, but massive growth is unlikely.

- The AN-Institutes collaborate with other partners within the technology transfer and innovation systems – outsourcing expertise where they do not have it themselves. Implicitly, then, they are an important part of the competition-collaboration dynamic that exists within German technology transfer.

- Structures are evolving within the Fraunhofer which maximise the synergies within the 47 institutes as demonstrated by the case study of TEG. Further, biotechnology monitoring and application R&D within the structures of the Fraunhofer combine with the collaborative approaches taken by separate technology transfer institutes and industrial partners both domestically and abroad. This ensures that any radical innovations, from whatever source, will be supported by the traditional, incrementally innovative, capacity of the German system to produce engineering solutions in the long run.

- Finally, the Fraunhofer as a whole attracted such a substantial amount of industrial funding in the year 1997/8 that the government (through the BMBF) increased its funding by five per cent for the year 1998/9. At a policy level, this demonstrates a commitment both to the Fraunhofer as a bridging institution and to the dual system of technology transfer and innovation.

Interim evaluation

The structures involved in German research and development and Science and Technology policy are so complex that it would not be feasible to suggest that the whole innovation system could be transferred to a British policy context. However, one common tenet of the social market economy generally and the innovation system in particular does have an appeal even in an era of tight budgetary control. A systematic dual funding structure such as is exhibited in the German system allows basic science to be transferred to end users on a non-competitive basis. Companies funding the two-third specific product and/or prototype development then have justified intellectual property rights over their research, which they are then free to exploit commercially.

The key to the German system, though, is not simply in this funding structure. It is in the historically close adherence to the structure across the whole innovation system, which has given companies the security to innovate on the foundation of common basic science transferred through the intermediate organisations like the Fraunhofer. In contrast to the market-based and voluntaristic British system, German technology transfer is systematic and carefully delineated: thus avoiding ugly disputes over ownership and commercialisation. And, while the structure of government funding is broadening, the principal of one-third funding still remains.

At the micro level of the technology transfer system, there are lessons that can be learnt from the experience of the Fraunhofer in a changing technological and commercial environment. The key is to create technology transfer organisations that can effectively link the science base with its commercial applications. The Fraunhofer has re-invented itself to account for current and future changes in its environment. This is not easy to engender within an organisation. But a policy that could inject this type of dynamism into British technology transfer, removing its retrospective and 'catch-up' tendencies, would be an effective and exciting policy indeed. This is not a question of money but rather a question of market-near *reflective* thinking.

The technology transfer system in the US

There is a substantial amount of technological activity in the US and American institutions dominate in radical innovations and hi-tech. This emanates from the unique features of its technology transfer system, which tends to favour long term innovation and basic research with strong market orientation. In the context of the British policy, therefore it is essential to examine these features and to extract any aspects that may inform the debate.

Features of the US technology transfer system

US research and development is massive. At around 2.5 per cent of GDP it is proportionately similar to the amount spent on R&D in Germany. However, taken in absolute terms (using a constant 1987 dollar calculation), the level of R&D spending is equal to the combined amounts spent in Germany, France, Japan and the United Kingdom added together (Abramason et al 1997 p62). There are three reasons for examining the system in some detail in a British policy context:

- Although it is commonly assumed that much of this research is conducted within the private sector, this hides an important, if discrete, role for government funding.

- The delineation between university and industry research is clear and the American system, perhaps contrary to expectations, is funded in a way that favours longer-term and collaborative research (Schmoch, 1999).

- The legal framework of patenting in the US has changed since the early eighties to increase the number of patents being registered by university professors (Abramason et al 1997, Schmoch 1999, Hill 1999). The result has been an increased profile for patenting activity within universities and, critically, an increased number of patents.

- Despite its size, the American R&D system produces radical innovations that are 'close to the market'.

The system is made complex by its size rather than by its structure. Table 6.4 shows the size of the R&D structure in the US in 1993.

Table 6.4 Numbers in the US R&D system (1993)	
Aspect of R&D system	Absolute numbers
Engineers and scientists	963,000
Companies	41,000
Federal research laboratories	720
Colleges and universities	875
Non-profit R&D performing institutions	2300
Source: Abramson et al 1997	

The market-based nature of the US economy is reflected in its technology transfer system which is grouped roughly into four sectors: government (federal, state and local), private sector (industrial), non-profit academic institutions (colleges and universities) and other non-profit institutions (research institutes and foundations). Three of these sectors fund R&D as well as conduct R&D as shown in Table 6.5 which shows the percentage of total funding for each R&D area classified by the source of funds in 1995. Although universities and colleges are R&D performers, they do not have their own funds for R&D and, hence, are not included in the table.

Table 6.5 Funding sources for specific areas of R&D in the US (1995) by %			
	Federal government	Industry	Other non-profit organisations
Basic Research	58	24.2	7.5
Applied Research	36	67	4.8
Development work	29	70.4	<2
Source: Derived from Abramason et al 1997			

What is of interest from Table 6.5 is the relatively high level of funding for basic research accounted for by the Federal Government and, similarly the high level of funding for applied research which stems from industrial sources.

Government funding at Federal, State and Local levels

The importance of defence spending in total government funding for R&D in the US is well known. Indeed, the decline in government spending over the last ten years in particular can be attributed partially to the end of the Cold War. Even so, government expenditure remains an important part of total R&D with funding for health related projects (as identified above) especially important. Some two-thirds of total federal government spending goes to support private research (Abramason et al 1997, p69).

Government funding at Federal, state and local level also goes to universities. Indeed, for State and Local governments, college and university funding represents their major R&D expenditures. Hence, the principal source of 'academic R&D dollars' is Government.

Private industry

In 1995 71 per cent of all US R&D was conducted in the private sector and, as such, is the single most important source both of R&D funds and of R&D itself. It would be tempting to regard this as a logical outcome of the market based system that operates within the US. However, there is a strong bias in favour of 'market over-riding' collaborative research and, interestingly, Federal government funded research. There are two structures within the US system which are of particular interest in the context of this 'market-override':

- Private Engineering Research Institutes, which focus on applied research as a response to the perceived absence of Federal government funding for this type of research. These institutes conduct collaborative, pre-competitive research. However, in reality the funding of these institutes is largely derived from public sources (in particular the Department of Energy and Department of Defence) – only 10-30 per cent of their funding comes from industrial sources. As the comparable figure for Fraunhofer institutes is 30-45 per cent, this is a relatively low proportion (Schmoch, 1997:18).

- Federal research laboratories have started to introduce industry-related applied research activities to facilitate technology transfer. Cooperative Research and Development Agreements (CRADAs) are used, again especially by the Department of Energy and industrial companies (or consortia). Under these types of agreement, consortia or clients suggest research projects to laboratories and in return expect the research to be conducted to their specifications. This is supposedly closer to the market than, for example, German laboratories that have to undertake partner-searches themselves (Schmoch 1997 p19).

Colleges and universities (non-profit-making)

Universities performed 12.6 per cent of all US R&D in 1995. They are a pillar of basic research in the US since even industry funded R&D at universities tends to be pre-competitive and 'blue sky' in nature. University R&D is particularly supported by two infrastructural factors:

- Flexible university organisational and administrative structures which facilitate and enable the establishment over the medium term of 'Centres' (UIRCs discussed below in more detail).

- A favourable patenting environment since the Bayh-Dohl Act in 1980. This Act gave the universities the right to patent, and hence commercially exploit, any inventions they developed using federal funding. The licenses granted were, under this Act, allowed to be exclusive and were thereby made more accessible to industrial licensing too (Schmoch 1999 p9).

University-Industry Research Centres (UIRCs)

Universities tend to be structured to facilitate an entrepreneurial orientation to research and this flexibility allows for industry oriented research centres (UIRCs) to be affiliated to and integrated into university structures relatively easily. For example, a group of academics develops a five-year research programme and acquires industrial sponsorship for it. The University will contribute up to 30 per cent of necessary funds to set up a dedicated UIRC, while the Federal Government (through the National Science Foundation) will contribute a further 35 per cent of the total budget (Cohen et al 1994). In 1990, UIRCs accounted for some 15 per cent of total university R&D (Cohen et al 1994). There are no studies more recent than the Cohen et al study that provide the degree of detail on UIRCs, but an informed estimate would be that their importance has increased since then (Schmoch 1998, 1999).

This leads to the hypothesis that university-industry links are stronger and more dynamic in the US than in Germany. And certainly, measured through the *nature* of R&D being conducted and through the geographical location of these UIRCs, this assertion would seem to have some validity. The vast concentration of UIRC work is in IT and biotechnology and the centres tend to be located in innovative 'clusters', as is illustrated by the case of biotechnology discussed briefly below.

However, the hypothesis cannot be unconditionally accepted. Figures for patenting and for total industrial contributions to the total R&D expenditures of universities are given in Table 6.6, with comparable figures for Germany.

Table 6.6 University-industry links measured through patents and funding in Germany and the United States (1997)		
	United States	*Germany*
Industrial contribution to total university expenditure on R&D	1980: 4% 1997: 7%	1980: 2% 1997: 8%
EPA patents emanating from research conducted in universities	1970: 200 1980: 450 1995: 1850	1970: 400 1980: 600 1995: 1240
Source: Derived from Schmoch 1999		

The evidence presented in Table 6.6 shows that university-industry links, measured through the proportion of total university R&D and through patenting activity has increased in both Germany and the US. But, as mentioned above, the patenting structure in US has changed since 1980, which may account for the proportionately large increase in patents relative to the increase in Germany. These patents tend to be focused in IT and biotechnology related areas (reflecting the research needs of industrial clients). But while there is a re-focussing of US research towards these hi-tech areas, and while there is an increase in patenting, this does not guarantee the quality of the research or the patents granted (Henderson et al 1994).

Further, there is an inherent bias towards small companies within the German system (Harding 1999) which is not replicated in the US case. UIRCs tend to be funded by large companies. The dynamic and hi-tech focus of UIRCs, then, originates from companies that arguably would have the capacity to conduct the research in their own laboratories but who, for market-based reasons, have chosen to outsource the R&D. This is quite different to the collaborative and small company focus of AN-Institutes in Germany.

A final comment on the funding of UIRCs points to an important, and transferable, feature, however. They tend to be funded over a longer time period, of five years, and through grants rather than through contracts. This means that is has both the time and the freedom to experiment which is essential to blue sky research even if ultimately it leads to patentable product or process applied technologies. Unlike their counterparts in Germany undertaking industrial research, American Professors within UIRCs are not bound by the specific deliverable outcomes inherent to shorter-term contracts with specific deliverables.

Other non-profit R&D performers

While these are a relatively small contributor to total R&D in the US, they do contribute funds, particularly to research in specific areas. Over 45 per cent of the non-profit making R&D performers are in the are of health and related technologies. This has the effect of further increasing and deepening the US comparative advantage in health-related biotechnology.

Clustering: regional centres of excellence

Perhaps the most significant aspect of the US system, however, is the 'clustering' of basic and applied research around Centres of Excellence (usually attached to leading regional universities). A typical biotechnology cluster will include UIRCs, research institutes, industrial research laboratories and/or industrial production, testing facilities (for example hospitals or clinics), a developed regional product market, access to a highly skilled and young workforce and, critically, a risk-friendly venture capital environment (Reger, 1997). The result of the dynamic interplay between these aspects is the production of high-quality research with a strong bias towards hi-tech and radical innovation.

Conclusions and comparison of US and German case: a discussion for British policy

While the governments can learn from one another's policies and performance, national systems of innovation are embedded within the legal, administrative and institutional structures of the countries from which they originate. Hence, any prospect for transferring one structure to another is highly limited. This does not preclude the possibility of individual parts of the systems being appropriate in another context, however. For example, German universities tend to have formal research links with industrial partners through contracts, which are relatively short term (around two years) and which usually have clearly specified deliverables. Further, the legal structure for patenting, which has not changed since the 1950s tends to be contradictory and does not necessarily create effective incentives for university professors to seek industrial partners. In contrast, the American system is longer term, based as it is on grants that are open-ended and flexible, usually over a five-year time span. The patenting structure that has developed since the Bayh-Dole act of 1980 has favoured innovations and has led to the four-fold increase of industry-owned patents over the period since its implementation.

Discussion in Germany has focused on means of introducing greater flexibility and incentive structures into the system and intensifying the research links between industry and universities. This is not to suggest, however, that the German system is inappropriate to an international economic order dominated by radical innovations and global companies. Indeed, the German structure, contrary to popular perceptions, has a strong internal dynamic through historically developed collaborative research networks. These networks favour the small and medium-sized companies in a way that existing structures in the US do not. Both AN-Institutes and Fraunhofer Institutes in Germany have been successful in radical innovations, with the AN-institutes in particular having a strong and developing role in biotechnology and information technology. Business start-ups, a technology transfer paradigm emanating from the US are developing in Germany with similar incentive structures and longer-term research foci. Some degree of separation and independence in each system is necessary, however, in order to ensure that 'blurring' of the distinction between scientific (basic) research and technological (applied) research does not result in a reduction in the intensity of pure, independent research. While there is no evidence of this as yet, institutional, legal and administrative structures must evolve to ensure this separation in both countries.

It is, then, in this 'bi-lateral' transfer between the knowledge based in scientific research and its product and process application that the essence of a successful technology transfer system lies. Contract research tends to favour one-way technology transfer where the contracted researcher is a 'supplier of knowledge' to its customer in the form of deliverable outputs. Collaborative research, ranked highly by university professors in both countries, means that knowledge exchange is a two-way process: universities transfer theoretical concepts to industry but equally learn from the research conducted by companies, which is often leading-edge in a particular discipline.

The format of this 'bi-lateral' knowledge exchange is complex and varies between the two countries. In America, informal networks are important in generating future projects and partners and in disseminating (and marketing) the results of current research. In Germany, formal and informal networks between universities and companies have existed since the beginning of the 19th century – this is essential in understanding how interactions are developing now. In both countries, collaborations and interactions are intensifying and, although there are grounds for some scepticism about the final level that such relationships should reach, there is evidence in both nations that an internal knowledge exchange dynamic creates innovations (Schmoch 1999).

Policy implications

British analysts and policy makers alike have tended to regard British R&D systems as closer to the United States model than to structures in Germany. This is a phenomenon of the last 20 years during which many of the institutions have become decentralised and market-based. But markets are not a substitute for effective policy towards R&D, as both the US and the German cases clearly demonstrate. In both cases, substantial amounts are given to public funded R&D, there are policies to encourage collaboration in innovation and the R&D is clustered in Centres of Excellence.

The US case in particular, however, suggests some interesting policy avenues worthy of further investigation:

- Despite the market based structure of the US R&D system, the general nature of basic research is funded by government (although not exclusively) while applied R&D tends to be funded by industry (although again not exclusively). This suggests that there is a delineation between public and private gain that is reflected in the balance of funding. In Britain, this balance is vaguely defined and rests largely on a voluntaristic approach to markets. At the heart of any R&D system, however, has to be a clear distinction in responsibility for funding.

- British policy should take account of the historical development of universities over time. From the US case, there is no reason to suggest that entrepreneurial/industrially based universities have greater or more effective links with industry than do their counterparts in a more co-ordinated/public sector model such as exists in Germany. British universities arguably resemble German structures more than American because of the way they have evolved in the State sector. Unlike German universities, however, their links with industry have traditionally been 'arms length'. Much has happened to alter this over the past 20 years, but many changes have been unsystematic and routed in the desire to reduce science and technology expenditure rather than increase it.

- Intricately bound with the nature of British universities is the way in which they are funded. Again, much has altered in the past 20 years and markets for research funds are highly contested. However, the US case demonstrates clearly that longer term funding through grants is a more effective means of producing hi-tech and radical research than is contract research with specific deliverables.

- Ownership of the results of research is important and the US case illustrates that favourable incentives for innovation can be created through the patenting and licensing system. In Britain this process can be extremely costly to individual entrepreneurs and researchers.

- Encouraging clusters of innovation with public and private funds in regional centres has produced dividends for the US technology transfer system. Evidence of such clusters is emerging in Britain too, but more could be done to stimulate these.

Ultimately, however, both the US and the German cases point to the usefulness of formal and informal networks, of education and training and of project management according to industrial principles in industry-HEI collaboration. Neither country faces the cultural difficulties experienced in the UK since partnership structures have evolved as part of the economic structures in the two countries. Even so, both systems have mechanisms to ensure that any mistrust is limited through networks and through partnership programmes. Clearly these are the basic lessons for British policy.

7. Conclusions and policy recommendations

The book started with a discussion of the context into which any analysis of HEI-industry links must be placed. It was argued that there are moves to create closer links, and that these interactions have the potential to increase productivity, to improve product and process innovation and, ultimately, to stimulate economic growth through improved company performance and through the creation of high-growth spin outs. A model was developed which was refined in subsequent chapters. A distinction was made between the types of 'business' programmes which result in radical innovations and spin outs (and which are perhaps more appropriate to fast growing technological areas like pharmaceuticals and biotechnology) and the 'partnership' programmes which are inherently more suited to incremental innovation within traditional sectors such as engineering and construction.

Partnership programmes have three inherent attractions, which are particularly important in the context of the policy discussion to be developed in this chapter. First, they are relatively low cost in that activities are intrinsically developmental and, as such, are funded largely through the private sector. Second, they provide the means to overcome the cultural difficulties that have plagued university-industry links in this country. In particular, such interactions have 'trust-building mechanisms' such as education and training, industry networks and personnel exchanges which are low risk and provide the basis on which the parties can develop mutual understanding. Finally, and most importantly, they are particularly suitable in generating the interest of small and medium-sized enterprises (SMEs) through participation in networks and courses.

It appears from the research, then, that there is a real need to sharpen the focus on these types of project through a specific *innovation policy*. Such a policy would recognise the importance of incremental innovation as a means of generating competitive advantage but would act as a prompt particularly to SME involvement in such linkages. Incremental innovation by definition produces improvements in productivity and product and process innovations, as the case material demonstrates. And, as the comparative material from Germany shows, there is no reason to suggest that an incremental innovation system necessarily is less dynamic or even less innovative than one geared up to radical innovation.

This is not to suggest that policy should ignore radical innovations or the university-industry links that produce high growth potential 'spin-out' companies. Indeed, it would be a grave mistake to neglect these and even Germany, for years renowned for its engineering-based innovations has, since 1996, spent vast amounts on prompting university spin-outs and hi-tech innovation. The US example illustrated the means by which such 'business' programmes can develop and policy has much to learn from this – particularly in the long term funding structures of University-Industry Research Centres (UIRCs).

This chapter, then, aims to synthesise the material from the research by developing the generic characteristics of successful collaborations between industry and the public sector research base. It then develops specific policy suggestions from this discussion.

Research conclusions

Creating a demand for innovation

The most fundamental barrier to the creation of university-industry links is firms' scepticism about the ability of such links to improve their business. The case studies, and especially the experience of Warwick Manufacturing Group (WMG), illustrate what universities can do to stimulate the demand for innovation and knowledge links. Key factors in this process are education and research synergies, but also of importance is the need to demonstrate quickly to firms the current and potential benefits of collaboration. This is best done by short-term contract research that has a good chance of early pay-off. Once this has been done successfully, and the company becomes more confident in the university's ability to deliver, there is a better chance that they will fund more speculative, pre-competitive work in the future.

This process of building up a research client base can be seen at work with EMC testing, where an initial piece of contract research with Rover Group led to a much larger piece of pre-competitive, collaborative research including Rover, its supply chain and a software development company. On a smaller scale, the Lanemark case study began with a piece of contract research which then led to further contact through the Managing Director teaching on WMG courses, a Teaching Company Scheme collaboration and the possibility of further research collaboration in the future.

University infrastructure

Most of the examples of successful links with business uncovered by this research have been found in universities with a strong *institutional* commitment to collaboration with industry. This has either taken the form of historically strong links which have been revitalised in the modern era, such as at Salford, or more recent developments associated with the need to deal with a funding crisis (Warwick) or due to the influence of a vice-chancellor (Sheffield). The AN-Institutes in Germany and the UIRCs in the US further illustrate the policy potential of university-based industrial research centres. The support of the local university is key in providing overhead support (buildings, electricity, lighting and heating etc), but when harnessed with industrially driven research, the potential for innovation is huge.

This suggests that, where universities are keen to encourage links with industry and to expand their economic development role, they should give consideration to the following factors:

● Altering their mission statements to give economic development explicit consideration alongside academic research and teaching.

● Concentrating decision-making in a streamlined, centralised body but then allowing relative autonomy to those units and centres it supports, along the lines of the Warwick model.

● Promoting a culture in which collaboration with industry is regarded as mainstream and good practice.

Incentive structures

Chapter One examined how academics are discouraged from engaging in applied work with industry because it does not lead to career enhancement in the way that excellence in academic research and teaching are inclined to do. Among the case studies, WMG is best able to overcome this problem, by providing industrially-relevant salaries and a career structure in which successful collaboration with industry is the primary determinant of advancement. WMG is only able to do this, however, because it has attracted a large group of partner companies who fund on a regular basis the Group's teaching and research activities. This work is paid for at rates sufficiently high to recruit and retain the types of researchers, who often have industrial experience, which WMG is looking for.

There is not a great deal which universities attempting to begin the process of industrial collaboration can learn from this approach since it would be very hard at an early stage to initiate a reward structure which exists independently of the normal academic arrangement because it is unlikely that the university would be able to attract a sufficient quantity of lucrative work to do so. WMG was only able to do this initially because of the up-front financial support that the University's Earned Income Group provided. It is probably necessary for state support, in the form of something similar to the recently initiated HEROBEC (Higher Education Reach-Out to Business and the Community) fund, to provide a kick-start to university-industry collaborations.

Even if it is possible for institutions to provide a reward structure for applied work, this needs to bear a sufficiently close relationship to the standard academic career path and, ideally, the industrial research and development (R&D) one, so that researchers can shift between different environments if they so choose and thus bring about the sort of cross-fertilisation which would be of benefit to all sectors.

A first step in this process is to elevate the relative standing of economic development in the university's mission statement. This does not have to imply parity of esteem between academic research, teaching and economic development although this would be useful if the university is committed to working with industry. This then makes it possible to create a legitimate and recognised career framework for academics, which rewards and gives status for work in application of research, complementary to the framework for those following careers in scholarly research and teaching. For this reward structure to enjoy parallels with that for industrial R&D, however, and thus make possible secondments and short-term placements that encourage cross-fertilisation between the different sectors, there would need to be quite a substantial uprating of the academic pay structure. These issues are dealt with in more detail below.

Intermediate institutions

Those examples of research collaboration between industry and the public sector research base that are analysed in this report suggest that intermediate institutions have a number of advantages over direct interaction between universities and industry. Intermediate institutions are relatively autonomous from both the science base and the business sector but provide a link between them. As such they are independent of each and can be 'impartial translators' as well as network organisers and project managers. Their motivation is commercial since large proportions of their total revenue are gained from industrial contracts.

The three examples in the context of this research are as follows:

- *Warwick Manufacturing Group:* The ability to deliver work, especially contract research within specified timescales and to specified targets rests on the fact that its staff are not trying to fit the collaboration with industry around their core tasks of academic research and teaching.

- *Medical Research Council Collaborative Centre:* Members are involved exclusively in industrially based research and operate without public support.

- *Fraunhofer Institutes:* The Fraunhofer Institutes in Germany operate as bridging institutions between the science base and its industrial application. Scientists conduct public and private sector research, but all is on a contract basis and, while some institutes publish, this is not a uniform feature of Fraunhofer Institutes.

The research would suggest that institutions, which are attached to the science base but relatively autonomous from it, are thus in a better position to undertake large-scale collaboration with industry than universities, which seek to engage in industrial links without forming intermediate institutions of this type. These intermediate institutes also appear particularly suited to incremental innovation because scientists are not based at the 'cutting edge' of blue sky research. Projects are therefore demand led and thus, by definition, meet the needs of industry. This degree of abstraction from the science base also guarantees the integrity of blue sky research.

Intermediate institutions or centres also bring other advantages. As they often gather expertise from more than one university, they can achieve a critical mass that makes for far more valuable interaction with industry than would be possible at one university. One of the best examples of this from our research is provided by the Virtual Centre of Excellence in Mobile and Personal Communications (Mobile VCE), which brings together seven universities in a highly effective collaboration with the leading mobile and personal communications companies operating in the UK. This factor is also well-illustrated by US experience, where the UIRCs and regional Centres of Excellence often combine expertise from a number of universities and, indeed, other institutions such as research institutes, industrial research laboratories and testing facilities.

One element of collaboration that is also evident in the US but surprisingly less so in the UK is the presence of centres which bring together different departments from within the same university. The Centre for Innovation in Product Development at MIT, for example, brings together the School of Engineering and Sloan School of Management. This contrasts starkly with the lack of collaboration between WMG and the Warwick Business School. This may be the result of funding structures in the UK, where the Research Councils support relatively few joint initiatives. An exception to this is the highly successful Innovative Manufacturing Initiative, which is funded by the Biotechnology and Biological Sciences Research Council (BBSRC), Engineering and Physical Sciences Research Council (EPSRC) and Economic and Social Research Council. More joint Research Council programmes like this may well encourage the development of multi-disciplinary intermediate institutions, to the advantage of UK companies, which collaborate with them.

Industrial relevance and industrial champions

The notion of 'focused blue sky research', used by the Edward Jenner Institute for Vaccine Research to summarise its orientation, neatly captures the need to carry out research which advances knowledge but which maintains at least some industrial relevance.

Where centres are carrying out strategic and applied research, the need to explore issues of interest to the industrial client base is obviously greater. Many of the centres analysed in this study were very successful in carefully involving their industrial members in the formulation of their research programmes, so they could lay genuine claim to being industry-led. This is a very important ingredient of successful university-industry collaboration, especially where firms are sceptical about the value of working with universities and suspect that universities are only interested in their own research agendas. The Sheffield Materials Forum (SMF) and the Construct IT Centre of Excellence, based at Salford University, are particularly good at teasing out from firms the research issues they want to investigate.

SMF and Construct IT also score highly in relation to another factor that makes for effective collaboration. This is the use of 'industrial champions', key figures from the industrial sectors involved in the collaboration who transfer their enthusiasm for it to their business contacts. Industrial champions of this nature use their credibility amongst firms, which academics in the first instance will usually not have, to overcome the scepticism that firms often exhibit before the collaboration becomes well established.

Education/research synergies

While WMG is noted for the huge volume of its research-based collaboration with industry, its educational provision has played a very important role in facilitating these research links. In the early 1980s, very few firms were interested in research collaboration with universities, at least in engineering, so WMG concentrated instead on trying to improve their skill base, in relation to which firms were more willing to admit there was a problem. They developed a club of about thirty companies, most of which were based in the West Midlands, and encouraged them to send graduates for post-experience education programmes. In contrast to the 'generalist' courses prevalent in business schools, these programmes provided management training grounded in the engineering context. Groups of Warwick staff were simultaneously attached to companies to support the graduates and help them to apply their knowledge effectively in the business environment. Member companies eventually started to supply staff members as visiting lecturers at WMG as trust began to develop between the university and the firms. These courses, which were the forerunners of WMG's current Integrated Graduate Development Scheme (IGDS), led eventually to the building up of a stock of managers in engineering firms who were responsive to the need for enhancements in the product base. Their presence thus made it feasible for research collaboration between WMG and the regional manufacturing base to occur.

This process of using education as a way of increasing demand for research links is one which WMG has practised for almost twenty years, and so has had time to reap the benefits. Most of the other collaborations we have looked at are much more recent in origin, but some of them, especially Construct IT, have made a promising start in using their IGDS to build up the industrial demand for knowledge links in the construction sector.

Managing the entrepreneurial vision

Carrying out successful links with industry requires the key players on the university side to have a wide range of skills and to carry out a number of challenging activities with which they are unlikely, in the first instance, to be familiar. They need to have an awareness of the transferable aspects of the knowledge base but also sufficient entrepreneurial vision to see the possibilities for commercial exploitation. This ability to 'look both ways' is uncommon, but is an essential requirement for Directors of intermediate institutions which are carrying out knowledge transfer. While this function has been carried out to a large extent by one person in the case of WMG and MRCCC, it should probably be performed by a small management team, rather than one individual. This team would need to combine the qualities of entrepreneurial vision, acquaintance with the latest developments in fundamental research, understanding of the commercial environment and the possibilities for exploitation of findings from the knowledge base, financial acumen and the organisational skills needed to manage the knowledge transfer process.

Regional clusters

The national and international case studies produced some evidence to suggest that universities can be the foci of 'clusters' of firms from particular industrial groupings. In the case of WMG, it is able to bring together firms from a wide range of manufacturing sectors and, while operating on both the national and international levels, provides fora through which companies based in the West Midlands can network and form links with each other. Furthermore, quite a large proportion of WMG's work, especially with Rover Group, encourages technological diffusion down the supply chain, which involves working primarily with companies in the region. On a smaller scale, such activities are also carried out by other case study institutions, especially SMF and the White Rose Faraday Partnership for Enhanced Packaging Technology (WRP).

Facilitating the development of regional clusters brings benefits for both firms and universities. WMG's supply chain work with Rover, and its collaborations with small firms promoted through the Manufacturing Excellence Initiative, make it possible for technological innovations to be spread amongst a much wider range of firms than would be possible if such clusters did not exist. The consequences of this for productivity and profitability are made clear by the SME case studies. This industrial learning is facilitated further by the development of inter-firm networks. For universities, developing industrial clubs is an essential part of building up the research client base and breaking down the barriers of scepticism which inhibit the formation of knowledge links.

Regional clusters were, however, by no means important in all of the collaborations looked at by this research. The MRCCC and Mobile VCE, for example, collaborate mainly with the leading companies in the pharmaceuticals/biotechnology and mobile/personal communications sectors respectively, and these are not concentrated in particular regions of the country (likewise with Construct IT in the construction sector). Clusters tend to be important where supply chain development is an important aim of the leading companies involved in university-industry interaction, as at Warwick, or where an industrial district provides a concentration of firms from a particular sector, as in Sheffield.

The formation of networks in the communications sector, however, and also to a lesser degree in construction, suggest the development perhaps of 'national clusters', where companies see the advantages of inter-firm links but do not share a particular regional location. Instead, they are brought together by groups of universities in virtual centres. Government industrial and regional policy on clusters needs to encourage this type of grouping as well as the more conventionally understood regional concentrations.

A notable feature of the regional clusters observed in this research is their existence in medium-tech rather than hi-tech sectors. Regional clusters of course exist in hi-tech sectors such as biotechnology and software development, and these clusters were those that the government committed itself to support in the Competitiveness White Paper. But there is a strong argument for regional clusters to receive some support outside of these sectors. The Warwick and Sheffield groupings are medium-tech but technological innovation plays a crucial role in enhancing firms' productivity and profitability. These companies tend to export a high proportion of their output and are employment-intensive compared to many hi-tech companies, which means they produce a lot of relatively well paid jobs, thus providing a connection between the 'improving productivity' and 'increasing employment' agendas.

Policy recommendations

While the conclusions outlined above show what universities and firms can learn from the research to encourage interaction, this section outlines the policy changes which government could bring about to provide it with further support and encouragement. The policy recommendations are divided into those which advocate enhancement of existing policies and provision, changes in the criteria by which potential projects are assessed under current programmes, and new initiatives.

Enhancement of existing policies and provision

Basic science

The case studies showed that business demand for collaboration with the public sector research base is greatest where university researchers are able to access the latest developments in basic science. It is not an overstatement to say that a high quality, curiosity-driven science base is the lifeblood of university-industry interaction. As such, this report welcomes the additional support given to the science base by the first Comprehensive Spending Review, but suggests that this should be the beginning of enhanced provision and not the final statement.

Higher Education Reach-out to Business and the Community (HEROBEC) Fund

Jointly created by the Department of Trade and Industry (DTI), Department for Education and Employment (DfEE) and Higher Education Funding Council for England (HEFCE) in 1999, the

HEROBEC Fund is for activities that will increase the capability of universities to interact with business to promote technology and knowledge transfer, strengthen higher skills development and improve student employability. It is intended to initiate a third stream of funding, to complement HEFCE's existing grant for teaching and research. As such, it provides financial support for the type of activities that this research has shown to encourage innovation and improvements in business performance.

A total of £11 million is earmarked for the Fund in 1999-2000, rising to £22 million in 2002-03. In similar moves, Scottish Enterprise and the Scottish Higher Education Funding Council will devote an extra £11 million per year over the next three years to these issues. While HEROBEC is clearly a welcome development, the scale of funding would need to be considerably higher to have an appreciable impact on universities' ability to work effectively with industry, especially with regard to English institutions. At the very least, the funding for English institutions should be equivalent *pro rata* to that provided in Scotland, which suggests the HEROBEC budget should rise to about £100 million by 2002-03.

Faraday Partnerships

It was announced in the 1998 Competitiveness White Paper that the DTI would be supporting the Faraday Programme introduced by the EPSRC in 1997, to the extent that the number of Faraday Partnerships would rise over the next two or three years from its present level of four to about twenty. This makes the Partnerships an important method of encouraging university-industry links to facilitate technology transfer. At the core of the Faraday model are Research and Technology Organisations (RTOs), which play the crucial 'translator' role in linking firms, especially SMEs, with the science base.

The basic structure of the Faraday model is supported by this research. The three actors in the Partnership – universities, intermediate institutions and companies – are each ascribed roles that are consistent both with their areas of expertise and functional capabilities. The universities provide high quality research capacity, the RTOs are able to 'translate' this for the benefit of the companies, and the companies feed in their knowledge of the specific conditions which apply in their sector, so that the research collaboration can produce industrially-relevant enhancements in product and process development. The use of RTOs as intermediate institutions alleviates much of the usual constraint on university-industry interaction applied by the need for university staff to do their teaching and academic research as well as industry collaboration. The RTOs can take most of the responsibility for project delivery, accessing expertise from a group of university researchers as needed.

However, the essential ingredients of Faraday as a model of interaction between business and the public sector research base are present in some of the other collaborations examined, even where an RTO is not involved. In the case of WMG, for example, most of the researchers are employed primarily to work with industry and thus are able to perform the function devolved to RTOs in the Faraday Partnerships. Likewise in the case of the MRCCC, the Centre staff play the 'translator' role between MRC fundamental research and pharmaceutical companies looking to develop new products unencumbered by the need to perform other activities. This suggests that, as DTI invites new applications for Faraday Partnerships, it should include proposals that allow for the intermediate institution role to be played by institutions other than RTOs.

Translators

Reference was made above to the need for Directors of intermediate institutions to 'look both ways' when facilitating knowledge transfer between universities and industry. Policies that help university staff to develop the entrepreneurial skills required by this task would increase the supply of potential 'translators'.

In this respect, the Science Enterprise Challenge, which has created eight enterprise centres at leading UK universities, will have an important role to play. The aim of the centres is to equip scientists and engineers with entrepreneurship and business skills to develop the transfer and exploitation of knowledge and know-how. The programme was introduced by the 1998 Competitiveness White Paper and £25 million of funding is allocated in the first instance. The eight centres were decided upon in September 1999 and the eight lead universities are Bristol, Cambridge, Glasgow, Imperial College of Science,

Technology and Medicine, London Business School, University of Manchester Institute of Science and Technology, Nottingham and Sheffield.

As with the HEROBEC fund, this programme is well-conceived but conservatively funded, in relation both to the number of centres created and the support made available to each. A four-fold increase in funding and a doubling of the centres supported would produce a more adequate supply of translators. The highly regarded Teaching Company Scheme could also have its 'translation' role made more explicit.

Changes in assessment criteria

The research suggests that government programmes designed to encourage collaboration between universities and business could be made more effective if certain factors were given more weight than at present when funding proposals are being assessed. This applies to HEROBEC, Faraday Partnerships, Science Enterprise Challenge and all of the other programmes described in Chapter 1.

University mission statements and infrastructural support

In view of the finding that strong commitment to the economic development function at the university level is an important determinant of successful interaction with business, it is recommended that the content of university mission statements and tangible evidence of support for collaboration from a senior level within universities be given more weighting in the assessment of funding proposals.

Involvement of industrial champions

The research suggests that the chances of university-industry interaction having a lasting effect on business performance are greatly enhanced if industrial 'champions' are used to involve senior managers in the collaboration. Universities that are able to demonstrate access to such industrial champions should be given credit for this in assessment criteria.

Education/research synergies

Education and training played an important role in several of the case studies in ensuring that companies had willingness to engage in research collaboration with universities and the ability to implement any technological innovations which emerged from this. The ability to demonstrate such linkages should be used to assess whether universities would provide good value for any public money they should receive to encourage interaction.

Links between science departments and business schools

The research noted that some of the most successful US examples of university-industry links came about where university business or management schools and science or engineering departments had come together to form a multi-disciplinary centre best able to deliver effective collaboration with business. UK universities have been much less inclined to do this: of the eight centres created by Science Enterprise Challenge, only one was a formal collaboration between a business school and science department. It is recommended that the formation of such collaborations be given due weight when assessing funding proposals.

New initiatives

Evaluation and accreditation of applied work

The Research Assessment Exercise (RAE), which rates the quality of work done by a department, is at present the sole evaluator of research done in universities. On the basis of the score received, the higher education funding councils allocate money to the institution to cover the costs of infrastructure, staff and to seedcorn exploratory work. The conduct of the RAE was recently subjected to extensive review, in preparation for the next exercise in 2001. One of the key points of contention was the inclusion of applied work. The funding councils argue that current methods fairly represent applied work. Other commentators, particularly universities that cover a wide range of such activity, do not believe so.

The RAE is inherently biased towards basic research, especially that which is most easily disseminated through traditional academic journals. It is the contention of this report, however, that this bias is correct, and that the RAE should continue to act primarily as a measure of the academic research capacity of university departments and the main way in which funds are distributed to finance this research. This conclusion stems from the wide body of research which shows the importance of basic science and the numerous occasions when conducting this research that interviewees from business stressed that the thing they wanted most from universities was original thinkers, trained by the best academic researchers on state-of-the-art equipment. This excellence in basic science is 'the goose that lays the golden egg' as far as technological innovation is concerned, and reforming the RAE in such a way as to divert funding and recognition away from the best academic departments would be in danger of killing it.

What is required, rather than drastic reform of the RAE, is to develop ways of evaluating and accrediting work done with industry through a separate evaluation mechanism. If one can roughly divide the mission statements of universities into three: fundamental and strategic research; teaching; and work oriented towards economic development, then there needs to be separate evaluation. Teaching quality, itself believed to have been downplayed by the focus on the RAE, is now being assessed by an evaluation mechanism designed, not to focus purely on outcomes, but on the processes and mechanisms in place to achieve quality results. Given that teaching is a pursuit of all universities, this creates a comparative assessment exercise independent of the RAE.

Extending the same argument to the third mission, there should be a similar 'audit' of activities related to work done with industry. It would probably be difficult and also counter-productive to separate skill development and training issues from applied research since these are often very tightly linked in a firm's needs. Again, there should be an evaluation of processes and mechanisms rather than direct outcomes. The evaluation of the exact outcomes of applied work and collaborative research on the competitiveness of localities or individual firms is extremely difficult to make. Some indicators of measures that can be used however, are set out in Cohen *et al* (1994) and in Goddard (1997). The content of such an assessment should be discussed by an appropriate group of people drawn from the universities and industry.

This assessment could be used as part of the evaluation criteria for the award of HEROBEC funds.

Applied work also needs to be accredited at the level of the individual. As was noted previously, university researchers need to be given more incentive to participate in applied work. This means applied work should be integrated more fully into career progression. The BBSRC suggest a point system whereby an individual can accumulate credits for work done in a variety of contexts which would be taken into account in an assessment of salary review or career development. For many people working on a series of contracts, this would be invaluable. There should also be more encouragement and accreditation for secondments of academics to industry. A variant of this model is currently being pursued and developed by various engineering institutes through points accumulated for continuous professional development. Scottish Enterprise (1996) also want to encourage greater recruitment of staff with industrial experience. They would like to see flexible contracts involving joint appointments with industry. This type of 'portfolio' career structure will only become workable if the pay gap between academic and industrial sectors is at least reduced.

Cluster working parties

The study adds to much recent evidence in suggesting that universities can play an important role by providing the focal point for clusters of innovative businesses. It thus welcomes the initiatives suggested by the 1998 Competitiveness White Paper for encouraging such clusters, including the focus on biotechnology and the need to consolidate the UK's European lead in the commercial exploitation of public sector research in this area. However, the study also finds evidence of nascent clusters in sectors that are not obviously hi-tech but where technological innovation plays a crucial role in enhancing firms' productivity and profitability. Such clusters exist, for example, among engineering and materials businesses in the West Midlands, many of which are SMEs and have profitable research partnerships with the University of Warwick. While welcoming the existing initiatives therefore, this report recommends that the cluster working party exercise on biotechnology, convened by the government earlier this year, be replicated for a number of medium-tech sectors, with a view to identifying clusters in particular areas of the country and investigating ways of supporting their development.

Regional and sectoral centres of excellence

Much of the analysis reported in this research points to the need for the development of collaborative centres which bring together a number of key players in the innovation process. These include:

- academic researchers carrying out high quality basic research, especially if it is 'focused blue sky';

- researchers from intermediate institutions, be they university or RTO-based, who have the expertise to access the findings of basic research and apply them in collaborative research with companies;

- R&D/senior managerial staff from the business sector who are keen to reform their product development strategies or production processes by carrying out technological innovation.

Those intermediate institutions analysed in this research have performed this function to some degree, but not on the scale or with the scope which would maximise the benefit for firms in terms of improved economic performance. Even WMG, which carries out interactions with industry on a very large scale, does not engage systematically with basic research to the extent that it should. Indeed, it does not even have strong links with the business school with which it shares a campus. The other centres covered by the study, while engaging in research links with industry to varying degrees, have not been able to approach the scale of operation achieved by WMG. The exception here is MRCCC, but as an intermediate institution supplying the pharmaceutical and biotechnology industry's demand for exploitation of MRC basic science, it is clearly an outlier in terms of its industry's research intensity.

The UK position contrasts quite strongly with that revealed by international comparisons. A notable aspect of the US system of technology transfer is the 'clustering' of basic and applied research around Centres of Excellence (usually attached to leading regional universities). A typical cluster will include university-industry research centres (intermediate institutions), research institutes, industrial research laboratories and/or industrial production, testing facilities (for example hospitals or clinics), a developed regional product market, access to a highly skilled workforce and, often, a risk-friendly venture capital environment. The result of the dynamic interplay between these aspects is the production of high-quality research with a strong bias towards hi-tech and radical innovation. The AN-Institutes in Germany, analysed in detail in Chapter Six, are also similarly placed at the centre of regional agglomerations of innovative expertise.

In the US case, UIRCs are able to gather these players around themselves, and in the process they engage systematically with basic research as well as linking with firms and other institutes. The UIRCs are themselves often multi-disciplinary, with the Centre for Innovation in Product Development at MIT, for example, bringing together the University's engineering department and business school. The Centres of Excellence have a complex funding and intellectual property rights system, but the basic, pre-competitive elements of research generally attract considerable public funding while the more near-market elements attract substantial amounts of industrial funding.

Developing a system of regional and sectoral Centres of Excellence in the UK would provide the opportunity to both widen and deepen the existing matrix of university-industry links. Bringing together a wider group of institutions and types of research capacity would mean that a greater range of expertise could be applied to the task of improving firms' innovative capacity. Adequate public funding of basic research carried out by the Centres and sliding-scale public funding of applied research, where larger companies would fund all or nearly all of projects from which they benefited but SME-related projects would receive public support, would help to deepen the relationships.

The government should aim to create ten regional or sectoral Centres of Excellence by 2002, each receiving an average of £10 million funding in the 2000-2002 period. As this research has demonstrated, not all industrial sectors are characterised by regional clustering. Therefore, some of the Centres would need to be national, and probably virtual, rather than regional. The expertise from DTI's existing work programmes on clusters and sectors would need to be brought together to decide what was appropriate in the case of each industry.

National Innovation Agency

Most of the conclusions outlined above relate to micro-level issues but there is a wider macro-level issue that permeates much of the research. Interviews with university researchers, members of company R&D departments and company managers suggested that many companies reject the need for technological innovation and therefore research collaboration with universities. This applied to large as well as small companies but was more prevalent in the low-tech than the high- and medium-tech sectors covered. It was especially pronounced in construction.

Where companies reject the need for innovation, this usually comes from the Board level rather than the R&D or technical departments. One of the key factors in the successful development of the Sheffield Materials Forum was its ability, in the face of considerable scepticism, to get the early support of managing directors and chief executives. Endorsement of university collaboration at the highest level was seen as important if the later detailed interaction between university researchers and company technical staff was not be to marginalised.

This suggests the need for a macro-level attempt to raise the profile of innovation. This would have to be aimed at senior management and would need to come from senior and respected figures in government, and from leading university and company practitioners who have brought about successful collaborations between universities and industry. If this type of exhortation could raise the demand for knowledge links, the micro-level policies outlined above may be able to make them more effective and their benefits more demonstrable.

This innovation 'big bang' is best ignited by the creation of a National Innovation Agency (NIA). This would be a government agency charged with the task of defining and co-ordinating UK innovation policy particularly to ensure the most effective exploitation of the science base. As such, it should be part of the DTI but relatively autonomous from it. As well as stimulating the demand for innovation, the NIA would co-ordinate the different elements of innovation policy outlined and suggested by this report, and introduce mechanisms through which the work of different institutions – Faraday Partnerships, Regional and Sectoral Centres of Excellence and other collaborative centres – could be used to inform that of the others. At the same time as co-ordinating these large programmes, it would need to rationalise what is widely seen as a confusing and overlapping series of smaller schemes promoting applied and collaborative work.

Such an organisation, combined with the other policy recommendations made by this report and existing best practice, would stimulate more effective knowledge links.

References

Abramason H, Norman B, Encarnacao J, Ried P and Schmoch U (eds) (1997) *Technology Transfer Systems in the United States and Germany: Lessons and Perspectives* Washington DC National Academy Press.

Anderson J and Fears R (eds) (1995) *Valuing and Evaluating: assessment of the value of R&D in creating national and corporate prosperity* Report on the second SmithKline Beecham Symposium.

Anderson R (1993) 'Can Stage-Gate Systems Deliver the Goods' in *Financial Executive* November-December.

Aouad G (1994) *ICON Final Report* University of Salford.

Aouad G, Brandon P, Brown F, Cooper R, Ford S, Kirkham J, Oxman R, Sarshar M, Young B (1996) *Integration of Construction Information (ICON): Final Report – Integrated databases for the design of construction and management of construction* University of Salford.

Ashworth J (1985) 'Universities and Industry: National and Institutional Perspectives' in *Oxford Review of Education* Vol 2 No 3.

Ball R, Jennings P and Lever P (1992) 'EMC testing Rover cars' in *Engineering Science and Education Journal* December.

BMBF (1996) *Bundesforschungsbericht* Bonn, Bundesministerium für Bildung, Wissenschaft, Forschung und Technology.

BMBF (1998) *Zur technologischen Leistungsf'higkeit der Bundesrepublik Deutschland* Bonn, Bundesministerium fÚr Bildung, Wissenschaft, Forschung und Technology.

Brandon P (1998) *Salford University: An Historic Industrial Partnership* University Of Salford.

Buxton A, Chapman P and Temple P (eds) (1998) *Britain's Economic Performance* Routledge.

Cantwell J and Harding R (1998) 'The Internationalisation of German R&D' *National Institute Economic Review* 1/98 No 163 pp99-115. London, National Institute for Economic and Social Research.

Carter N (1982) *An improved susceptibility test for the EMC testing of aerospace equipment* Royal Aerospace Establishment (Farnborough, UK) TechnicalMemo, August.

Casper S (1998) 'National Institutional Frameworks and High-Technology Innovation in Germany – the Case of Biotechnology' unpublished paper to 'Innovation Systems and Industrial Performance' workshop, Wissenschaftszentrum, Berlin, 23-24 October 1998.

Centre for the Exploitation of Science and Technology (1995) *Bridging the Innovation Gap* CEST.

Cohen W, Florida R and Goe W (1994) *University-Industry Research Centres in the United States, Centre for Economic Development* Carnegie Mellon University.

Construction Task Force (1998) *Rethinking Construction* DETR.

Cooper R (1993) *Winning at New Products: Accelerating the Process from Idea to Launch* Addison-Wesley Publishing Company.

Cooper R (1994) 'Third-generation New Product Processes' in *Journal of Product Innovation Management* Vol 11.

Cooper R and Kleinschmidt E (1991) 'New Product Processes at Leading Industrial Firms' in *Industrial Marketing Management* Vol 20.

DTI (1997) *The Realising Our Potential Awards Scheme (ROPA): A Survey of Research Attitudes* DTI.

DTI (1998a) *Higher Education Winning with Business* DTI.

DTI (1998b) *Differences in companies' performance: British industry's under-Performing tail* Industry Economics and Statistics Unit, DTI.

DTI (1998c) *Our Competitive Future: Building the Knowledge Driven Economy* DTI Competitiveness White Paper.

The Economist (1995) 'The professor of product development' November, p120.

Edward Jenner Institute for Vaccine Research (1998) *Annual Report.*

Elliot C (1999) *Intellectual Property Rights – a Discussion* unpublished mimeo, June.

Faulkner W and Senker J with Velho L (1995) *Knowledge Frontiers: Public Sector Research and Industrial Innovation in Biotechnology, Engineering Ceramics and Parallel Computing* Oxford: Oxford University Press.

Finegold D and Soskice D (1988) 'The Failure of Training in Britain: Analysis and Prescription' in *Oxford Review of Economic Policy* Vol 4 No 3.

Gann D (1991) 'Technological change and the internationalisation of construction in Europe' in Freeman C, Sharp M and Walker W (eds) *Technology and the Future of Europe* Pinter.

Goddard J (1997) *Universities and Economic Development* Newcastle School of Management, University of Newcastle upon Tyne.

Griffin A and Houser J (1996) 'Integrating R&D and Marketing: A Review and Analysis of the Literature' in *Journal of Product Innovation Management* Vol 13.

Harding, R (1999) 'Standort Deutschland: An End to the Economic Miracle?' in *German Politics* April.

Hicks D and Katz J (1996) *UK Corporate Research Collaboration, 1981-1994. BESST Phase II: Final Report* STEEP Report, SPRU, University of Sussex.

Hohn, H (1998) *Steurungsprobleme und kognitive Strukturen der Forschung: Kernphysik und Informatik im Vergleich* Köln, Max Planck Institut für Gesellschaftsforschung.

Hohn, H und Schimank U (1990) *Konflikte und Gleichgewichte im Forschungssystem: Aktuerkonstellationen und Entwicklungspfade in der staatlich finanzierten ausseruniversit˜ren Forschung* Frankfurt, Campus Verlag.

House of Commons Select Committee on Science and Technology (1997) *The Innovation-Exploitation Barrier* The Stationery Office, HL Paper 62.

Kagioglou M, Cooper R, Aouad G, Hinks J, Sexton M and Sheath D (1998) *Final Report: Generic Design and Construction Process Protocol* University of Salford.

Kluth, M and Andersen, J (1997): 'Pooling the Technology Base' in Howells, J and Michie, J (eds) *Technology, Innovation and Competitiveness* Aldershot, Edward Elgar.

Krull, W and Meyer-Kramer F (1997) *Science and Technology in Germany* The Cartermill Guides. London, Cartermill Publishers.

LaPlante A and Alter A (1994) 'Corning, Inc: The Stage-Gate Innovation Process' in *Computerworld* October.

Lyall (1993) *The 1993 White Paper on Science and Technology: Realising Our Potential or Missed Opportunity?* MSc dissertation, Science Policy Research Unit, University of Sussex, Brighton.

Martin B and Salter A with Hicks D, Pavitt K, Senker J, Sharp M and von Tunzelmann, N (1996) *The Relationship between Publicly Funded Basic Research and Economic Performance* A SPRU Review, Report prepared for HM Treasury, SPRU, University of Sussex.

Mason G and Wagner K (1998) *High Level Skills, Knowledge Transfer and Industrial Performance: Electronics in Britain and Germany* Unpublished paper to 'Innovation Systems and Industrial Performance' workshop, Wissenschaftszentrum, Berlin, 23-24 October 1998.

NCIHE (1997) *Higher Education in the Learning Society, Report of the National Committee* The National Committee of Inquiry into Higher Education, NCIHE/97/850.

O'Connor P (1994) 'FROM EXPERIENCE: Implementing a Stage-Gate Process: A Multi-Company Perspective' in *Journal of Product Innovation Management* Vol 11.

OST (1997) *The Quality of the UK Science Base* OST, London.

OECD (1999) *Science, Technology and Industry Scoreboard* OECD.

Oulton N (1996) 'Workforce Skills and Export Competitiveness' in Booth A and Snower D (eds) *Acquiring Skills* Cambridge University Press.

Porter M (1998) 'Clusters and the New Economics of Competition' in *Harvard Business Review* November-December.

POST (1997) *Science Shaping the Future? – Technology Foresight and its Impacts* POST.

POST (1998) *Innovation from the Science Base* POST.

Prais S (1995) *Productivity, Education and Training* National Institute of Economic and Social Research.

Schmoch U (1998) *Interaction of Universities and Industrial Enterprises in Germany and the United States – A Comparison* Unpublished paper to 'Innovation Systems and Industrial Performance' workshop, Wissenschaftszentrum, Berlin, 23-24 October 1998.

Scottish Enterprise (1996) *Technology Ventures: Commercialising Scotland's Science and Technology.*

Senker J (1998) *Rationale for Partnerships: Building National Innovation Systems* Paper for STI Review, SPRU, University of Sussex.

Senker J (1999) *University Research Financing* Report prepared for the OECD, SPRU Science and Technology Policy Research University of Sussex February.

Sharp M (1991) 'Pharmaceuticals and biotechnology: perspectives for the European Industry' in Freeman C, Sharp M and Walker W (eds) *Technology and the Future of Europe* Pinter.

Sharp M and Patel P (1996) *Europe's Pharmaceutical Industry: an Innovation Profile* Draft prepared for DG XIII – D-4, April.

Simpson H (1998) *Biotechnology and the Economics of Discovery in the Pharmaceutical Industry* Office of Health Economics.

Skingle M (1998) *Developing effective partnerships between industry and academia* Glaxo Wellcome.

Schmoch U (1997) *Interaction of universities and industrial enterprises in Germany and the United States – a comparison* Unpublished mimeo.

Schmoch U (1999) 'Interaction of universities and industrial enterprises in Germany and the United States – a comparison' *Industry and Innovation* Vol 2 issue 1.

Technology Foresight Group (1995) *Progress Through Partnership* Report from the Steering Group of the Technology Foresight Programme, OST.

Technologie Nachrichten (1998) March, Hamburg.

Teaching Company Scheme (1997) *TCS Quinquennial Review: Report of the Review Panel and the Government's Response* TCS.

Warwick Network (1998) Warwick Manufacturing Group, Spring.